TWENTIETH CENTURY
INTERPRETATIONS
MAYNARD MACK, *Series Editor*
Yale University

NOW AVAILABLE
Collections of Critical Essays
ON

THE ADVENTURES OF HUCKLEBERRY FINN

ALL FOR LOVE

THE GREAT GATSBY

HAMLET

HENRY V

THE ICEMAN COMETH

SAMSON AGONISTES

THE SOUND AND THE FURY

TWELFTH NIGHT

WALDEN

TWENTIETH CENTURY INTERPRETATIONS
OF
THE FROGS

TWENTIETH CENTURY INTERPRETATIONS
OF

THE FROGS

A Collection of Critical Essays

Edited by

DAVID J. LITTLEFIELD

Prentice-Hall, Inc. *Englewood Cliffs, N. J.*

Current printing (last number):
10 9 8 7 6 5 4 3 2 1

Contents

PART TWO—*View Points*

TWENTIETH CENTURY INTERPRETATIONS
OF
THE FROGS

Introduction

by David J. Littlefield

We do not possess much reliable information about the life of Aristophanes. Other than perhaps a susceptibility to hiccups (the spasm which seizes him in Plato's *Symposium* may represent more than merely a flourish of comic characterization), most of what we know about him is drawn from things he says about himself in the comedies. But since these statements appear often in contexts that are either comical or ironical or both, it is hard to know how far they may be trusted. Consider, for example, this excerpt from the *Clouds*, probably written in 423 or 422 B.C., about his 'youthful' work, the *Banqueters*, produced four or five years earlier. The translation, a fine one, is by William Arrowsmith:

. . . I still remember that glorious day when the Judges—
men of whose extraordinary taste and discrimination it is a joy to speak—
awarded the First Prize to my youthful comedy, the *Banqueters*.
Now at that time, gentlemen, my Muse was the merest slip of a girl,
a tender virgin who could not—without outraging all propriety—
give birth. So I exposed her child, her maiden effort, and a stranger
rescued the foundling.

To a biographer this reference to the youthfulness of the poet's muse suggests that Aristophanes was very young when the *Banqueters* was performed in 427, and the passage has in fact been used to support the claim that Aristophanes was born in 445 B.C. The reasoning of the ancient biographers who made the claim ran something like this: famous men achieve notable successes in their fortieth year; Aristophanes' *Frogs* not only won first prize but it gained the unparalleled distinction of being performed—by official request—twice; it was performed in 405; ergo, Aristophanes was born in 445. This is the sort of reasoning that in ancient times was used to make Aristophanes a teenage genius. It is hard to reconcile this interpretation of evidence with the complaint Aristophanes makes (later in the same passage from the *Clouds*) that his fellow comic-dramatists have been having excessive fun at his expense teasing him about his baldness! It is safer to suppose that he was born in the decade 460-450, probably toward the end of it. But we do know for sure, because there are precise references to or extant citations from them, that Aristophanes wrote more than forty plays, eleven of which have survived in their entirety. These eleven, plus the recently discovered *Dyskolos* of Menander, are the only complete Greek comedies which have come down to us from antiquity. The first of them is the *Acharnians*, which was performed in 425 B.C. and won first prize. Because the play's topics, issues, and attitudes are in many ways characteristic of the art and outlook of Aristophanes, it is worth while to make a brief summary of its plot and salient features here. The hero of the *Acharnians* is Dicaeopolis, a rather querulous old farmer whose name means Mr. Just Citizen. He is tired of the Peloponnesian War which has been going on for six years without significant results, and he is tired too of the highly publicized, expensive, but futile diplomatic efforts to bring the fighting to a conclusion, so he negotiates his own private truce. His success in securing a separate peace immediately brings down upon him a screaming corps of militant charcoal-burners from the populous precinct of Acharnae, who proceed to abuse him for his treasonous, un-Athenian action. Confronted by this irrational mob, Dicaeopolis realizes that he will need to add affective and rhetorical tricks to the force of reasonable argument for his own verbal defense. He slips off to the house of Euripides to borrow a set of princely rags guaranteed (by Euripides' frequent and presumably successful use of this device of costume in several of his tragedies) to win the sympathy of even the most hostile audience. The speech he finally delivers wins over a portion of the Acharnians, and the remainder are persuaded his is the better side by the behavior of Lamachus, a strident, hawkish Athenian general who blunders onto the stage at that moment, demonstrating both his militancy and his stupidity. Once the Acharnians are convinced of his moral right to peaceful existence, Dicaeopolis begins to exploit its commercial possibilities. He sets up a marketplace and proceeds to deal in war-scarce goods with traders from Megara and Boeotia. For Megarian 'pigs' (actually a farmer's daughters in disguise), he exchanges salt and garlic, and for Boeotian birds and Copaic eels he trades an informer, one whose business it is to go about spying on his fellow citizens and betraying them to city officials—a special and unique product of wartime Athens so the play implies. The comedy ends as Lamachus limps howling in from the front lines wounded, while Dicaeopolis rolls exuberantly home from a banquet, singing and boisterous, with a pretty party-girl on each hand.

In his other plays Aristophanes comically explores many essentially similar issues, attitudes, and situations. Throughout his career he took a vigorous, articulate interest in the uses of rhetoric and the arts of public persuasion as well as those who taught them; in drama and dramatists and their impact upon the life of the city; in commerce and the political life of Athens; in the military activities of the city throughout the war and the generals and politicians who conducted them; and, finally, in any conspiracy of higher concern which threatened the right of the individual to engage in a full, free, and joyous life of the senses. The *Knights* in 424 was a bitter attack upon Cleon, the demagogue who had successfully purloined from his commanding general the public honor of having won the battle of Sphacteria-Pylos. The *Clouds* in 423 was an attack on the New Learning through its best known, and therefore most easily caricatured, public figure, Socrates. In 422 the *Wasps* exposed to comic scrutiny Cleon's shameless manipulation of the Athenian jury system. In 421 *Peace* parodied Euripides' *Bellerophon* and dramatized Athens' readiness for the Peace of Nicias, that uneasy hiatus in the Peloponnesian War which lasted for only a year. The *Birds* was performed in 414, and though no relationship is expressed in the play between the imperial ambition of its hero and the Athenian dream of empire then being pursued in Sicily, it is unlikely that the Athenians who saw the original production needed to have it pointed out.

The *Lysistrata* of 411 is a surprisingly lighthearted and good-natured peace protest, especially remarkable considering the full extent of the disaster which had occurred in Sicily in the years immediately preceding, and was just becoming fully known and felt at home in Athens. The sight of women from all over Greece cooperating in a sex-strike (which forces the men to give up their military madness and establish genuine peace throughout the lands and cities afflicted by the Peloponnesian War) must have struck the war-weary citizens of Athens as very poignant—and very saucy. The *Thesmophoriazusae*—the title means Women Celebrating the Feast of Demeter— was performed the same year as *Lysistrata* and also gives expression to a female point of view, but of a very different sort. Furious at the way in which Euripides presents the women in his plays as bibulous, lecherous, and self-serving creatures of passion, Aristophanes' ladies, on an exclusively female festival day, put the absent poet on trial and are moving swiftly toward his condemnation when there rises to his defense —carefully plucked, shaved, clothed and coiffed for the occasion—Mnesilochus, Euripides' kinsman, a male in disguise, who is soon discovered for what he is but who conducts a marvellously adroit defense of himself through parody of great trial scenes from Euripides' tragedies.

The *Ecclesiazusae* was probably performed in 392, a dozen years after the end of the Peloponnesian War and toward the end of Aristophanes' career. In it women in men's clothing take over the legislative assembly

of the city and create an entirely new system of laws. The results—a
government of the women, by the women, and for the women—are to
an extent predictable but enormously funny. The last play of Aristophanes, the *Plutus,* bears the name of the god of wealth, who is a
principal (and symbolic) character in the drama. He has in the past
distributed his gifts erratically and with little attention to the merit
of recipients because he is blind. The play is a dramatization—with
strong moral overtones—of what happens when his sight is restored.
There are records which indicate that after the *Plutus* Aristophanes'
son Araros produced two more of his plays which are now lost. On the
basis of this evidence most scholars have concluded that Aristophanes
must have died shortly after the *Plutus* was performed in 388.

II

The *Frogs* was performed, as we have seen, in 405. It possesses,
among its other distinctions, the honor of being the last—and very
likely the finest—extant specimen of Old Comedy, a form which dis-
appeared, along with Athenian democracy, upon the victory of Sparta
over Athens at the end of the Peloponnesian War in 404. Like Athenian democracy, Old Comedy has been more widely esteemed than
understood. Among ancient critics the term was employed to distin-
guish between the comic drama written in Athens in the 5th century,
most notably by Cratinus, Eupolis, and Aristophanes, and the New
Comedy of Menander, whose famous plays of the end of the 4th and
the early years of the 3rd century provided models for Plautus and
Terence. From these later writers of Roman comedy derive the stereo-
type characters, situations, and plots which ever since have characterized comic drama in the Western literary tradition. The ancients distinguished a Middle Comedy, too, but of this transitional form very
little is known; the *Ecclesiazusae* and *Plutus* are early (and the only
extant) examples of it.

For modern readers one distinctive feature of Old Comedy is its
chorus of actor-singer-dancers, usually twenty-four in number. The
entrance of this chorus through the passageway at the side of the
theatre called a *parodos* (πάροδος)—the name is applied also to the
entrance-song of the chorus—was often an immensely impressive
affair. Intricate dance movements, elaborate song arrangements, and
ornate costumes were sometimes combined, as in the *Birds,* to win
favor through sheer imaginative spectacle. Sometimes, as in the *Knights,*
the staccato rhythm of approaching military horsemen promised vio-
lence and engendered fear; sometimes an ethereal lyric fancy predominated, as in the entrance-song of the chorus of the *Clouds.* Often, as in

the case of each of these plays, the principal chorus gave its name to the comedy.

In this respect the *Frogs* is unique—it has two unrelated choruses: the "swan-frog" chorus which vocalizes while Dionysus and Charon row, row, row their boat across Lake Acheron, and the Chorus of Initiates, which Dionysus and Xanthias encounter after they have reached the underworld. The first is probably an off-stage chorus and is heard but not seen by the audience; at least this is the view (despite excellent suggestions for staging the entrance of a frog-chorus offered by David Barrett in his essay in this volume) which has generally prevailed among scholars. In contrast to the raucous song of the first chorus is the solemn and awe-inspiring entrance of the Chorus of Initiates. Their lyric invocation of Iacchos precedes a call for holy silence and the warning off of all profane persons. A reverent supplication of Demeter leads into a merry, second invocation of Iacchos, and their long, intricate song ends with a castigation of persons whose violation of morality has given public offense. In view both of its complex character and the fact that it introduces a second choral opening-song, this actual entrance on stage of the chorus, this true *parodos* of the *Frogs*, has generated a great deal of scholarly interest and some controversy. Three essays in this volume, those of Messrs. Lapalus, Mylonas, and Tierney, are devoted almost exclusively to elucidation of the possible meanings of the *parodos*, and many of the other essays in this collection comment upon or assume its significance.

A second prominent activity of the chorus is the delivery of the *parabasis* (παράβασις). An audience accustomed to attending performances of Old Comedy knew that at some point, usually about halfway through the play, the chorus would drop, partially or completely, its dramatic role to *turn to*[1] the audience in order to address it directly on one or more matters of topical interest. Politics or diplomacy; teachers, artists, poets, playwrights; economic, social, moral or cultural issues—any of these might be among the subjects reviewed by the chorus at this point in the play. The *parabasis* of the *Frogs*, as many of the essays in this volume note (Maurice Croiset examines it in detail), is the poet's earnest plea to the citizens of Athens to forgo faction, party allegiance, social and economic jealousy, personal animosity, and vindictive recrimination at a time when the city seemed to be—as in fact it was—at the point of ultimate peril after twenty-six years of war. It was this reasonable, proportionate, and tolerant appeal that won for the *Frogs* the unparalleled honor of a command second performance.

---

[1] The Greek verb is *parabainein*, hence the term *parabasis*.

In addition to the *parodos* and the *parabasis* of the chorus, the *agon* (ἀγών) is another distinctive feature of Old Comedy. The word denoted originally an assembly to watch games. The term came to be used to refer to the games themselves and eventually to almost any public contest, conflict, or competition conducted according to accepted rules. A debate or an action at law, for instance, could be called an *agon*. In Old Comedy the term refers to that portion of the play in which a formal debate, argument, or contest takes place.[2] Dicaeopolis' dispute with the outraged charcoal-burners in the *Acharnians* is an *agon;* it is a contest which observes rules of procedure. That is why Dicaeopolis employs the dramatic and rhetorical tricks he picked up from Euripides: they give him an edge in the game. Often in the plays of Aristophanes the *agon* precedes the *parabasis,* and the hero in the latter half of the play joyously reaps the fruits of his earlier victory. In the *Frogs,* however, the *agon,* a prolonged literary competition, comes after the *parabasis* and occupies most of the second half of the drama. This anomaly has generated a good deal of comment on the play's structure and unity—or the lack of it. Those who in this volume have addressed themselves to a consideration of the unity of the play—Messrs. Lapalus, Segal, and Whitman—argue, each for his own reasons, that disparate though the elements of the play may sometimes seem, they nevertheless do achieve final unity.

The contestants in the *agon* of the *Frogs* are Aeschylus and Euripides, two of the great tragedians of all times. What is Aristophanes' attitude toward them? And toward their tragedies? What is the social function of the dramatic poet? Even though the play pokes some rather sharp fun at Aeschylus, most readers have felt that Aristophanes respected him and the values expressed in his plays. About his attitude toward Euripides there is less agreement: some hold that Aristophanes must surely have hated a man he exposed as an object of scorn and whose plays he ransacked for purposes of derisive parody—look at the *Acharnians,* the *Frogs,* and the *Thesmophoriazusae.* Others—among them Gilbert Murray and G. M. A. Grube in essays in this volume—recognize that Aristophanes' parodies of Euripidean tragedy require a detailed knowledge of the poetry and of the poetic and dramatic techniques of the plays, arguing that this kind of knowledge may have been founded just as much upon respect and grudging admiration as

---

[2] The study of both the *agon* and the *parabasis* in Old Comedy is a very complicated matter to which scholars have devoted a great deal of time and energy. They have discerned in both an *epirrhematic* (balanced-speech) structure. The metrical symmetry of a portion of the *parabasis* known as an *epirrhematic syzygy* provides the basis for this kind of investigation. *Der epirrhematische Agon bei Aristophanes* by Thomas Gelzer (Munich, 1960) is an excellent recent study of this sort.

upon contempt and unmitigated distaste. Comic caricature expresses homage as much as disdain, they say, and I think they are right. But no matter what Aristophanes' attitude toward Euripides may have been —and what it really was we of course will never know—this competition between Aeschylus and Euripides is generally considered to be the first sustained and implicitly systematic criticism of poetry in Western literature. The essays of G. M. A. Grube and Gilbert Murray investigate the nature and importance of the practical criticism, and Bruno Snell's essay comments on the general critical position of the play as well as the moral and philosophical attitudes of Aristophanes which fostered it.

III

Isolating the distinctive elements of Old Comedy is a good deal easier —and safer—than risking opinions about its fundamental nature and possible meanings. But since one of the quixotic charms of literary criticism is a readiness to undertake the impossible, I shall attempt to identify what I take to be the essential components of a complex form by relating it to a distinctive phenomenon of our times: the happening. As I see it, Old Comedy is a 'plotted' happening, with both the dramatic and deliberative senses of *plotted* fully intended.[3] That is, Old Comedy creates a heightened sense of community by collocating seemingly random, often familiar elements which achieve—through apparently spontaneous interaction—a definite rhythm of progression and, finally, a coherent shape. Or, put another way, Old Comedy successfully combines elements so diverse that their union seems logically impossible, and in so doing creates or refurbishes a tight little society's sense of itself. In Old Comedy a sequence of improbable events becomes the pattern of inevitable action.

The *Frogs* is our example ready to hand and it is indeed a rich mixture of familiar components in surprising combinations. The principal action of the comedy is the descent of the main character into the underworld to retrieve from the land of the dead a lost loved one. The motif is familiar: Orpheus and his attempt to regain Eurydice comes immediately to mind, as do Theseus, Heracles, and Odysseus, who, each for his own reason, descended into the underworld; and it also summons to mind the qualities necessary to carry out the descent: heroic imagination, physical courage, craftiness, and adroit performance. But in the *Frogs* who is the hero who descends into the underworld?—an effete Dionysus. Whom does he seek?—the late, clever,

---

[3] The views which follow summarize ideas presented more fully in the editor's forthcoming '*The Fireworks of Destruction*': *A Study of Aristophanes' Frogs.*

tragic poet, Euripides. What is his armor?—a borrowed lion-skin and cudgel, neither of which he manages very well. Through what hazards and adventures does he gain entry to the underworld?—he solicits the advice of his half-brother Heracles, whom he has chosen to imitate, receiving from him information about routes, rest-stops, bars, brothels, restaurants, and so forth. Thus Dionysus, with a servant to tend the baggage, sets bravely forth! The witty mock-heroic manipulation of expectation with which the play opens is brilliant; it evokes unconstrained laughter, and it prepares the way for further displays of improbability and versatility. Songs of religious ecstasy, scenes of sheer slapstick, speeches of serious political and social commentary, parody, frolicking farce, and moral exhortation follow, flow into and around each other, are assimilated into and become the total drama. The diversity of elements is dazzling; their coexistence in a single work is startling, their fusion incredible. What, then, holds the play together?

In his essay on the opening of the *Frogs* Leo Strauss notes that only in this play of Aristophanes do we at the outset see and hear a god. Étienne Lapalus makes an elaborate defense of the divinity of Dionysus. Charles Paul Segal finds in the development of this multivalent god the source of the unity of the play. By incorporating into himself the manifold experiences of the drama, Dionysus reconciles their incompatible aspects, reaches a secure sense of self, affirms a system of values, and emerges as the embodiment of a renewed and unified city. Mr. Segal's argument is an impressive one: Dionysus is the chief actor of the drama, he is the god of theater, the master of many roles, and insofar as the experiences, attitudes, and values of the play can cohere in one person, they are unified in him. Cedric H. Whitman's view of the *Frogs* is in certain respects an extension of the thesis argued by Mr. Segal. Mr. Whitman sees in Dionysus "the collective selfhood of Athens, a selfhood all but lost to its own identity and seeking to recover it by a spiritual journey into Hell." His meticulous, perceptive, and persuasive explication of the play goes beyond an examination of character to express the view that the *Frogs* gives substance to an idea of Athens which is both comic and tragic, immanent and transcendent, historical and essential. In his view the redemptive power of initiation into the sacred mysteries is very important; correspondingly, there is a diminution of emphasis on the exercise of critical intelligence in the *agon*. My own view, which derives more from an attention to the essential mode of the play than to principal actor or central idea, would argue for a balance—in tension—between these forces of mystery and intellect.

There are in the *Frogs*, to examine briefly just one of its aspects, many judges, and many judgments are sought and rendered. At the very outset of the play Xanthias judges the jokes of Phrynichus, Lycis, and Ameipsias. Before long Heracles pronounces judgment on Iophon, Agathon, Pythangelus, and Xenocles. Charon on the shore of Lake Acheron discriminates between Dionysus and his slave, and on the other shore Xanthias has—or at least pretends to have—rare powers for discerning the threat of those phantasmagoric monsters he says he sees. Aeacus, one of the three chief justices of Hades, is called upon to decide which of the pretenders really is the divine Dionysus. He flails and fails and turns the problem over to Pluto and Persephone. The *parabasis* asks the citizens of the city to make careful judgments about its leaders—and all of these invitations to judgment are a prelude to the extended competition between Aeschylus and Euripides which Dionysus is asked to judge. But there is still another level of active judgment sought and presumably gained. In the *parodos* and the *parabasis* there are overt and covert appeals to the audience in attendance to judge this comedy the best of those offered it this day. The judges and judgments of the play exist to be submitted for judgment to the audience. In this paradox of the judged-judges and -judgments, Aristophanes' artistic strategy is made manifest.

The assembled citizens of Athens are asked to engage simultaneously in at least two activities: they are asked to involve themselves in the judgment-making activities of the drama (over which they have no control) in order that they may make a favorable judgment on the artistic merit of the play (over which they are assumed to have absolute control). The play's invitation to involvement begins in its opening lines—Xanthias asks Dionysus if he may tell a joke at which the audience never fails to laugh—and continues to its conclusion. Since the play is itself in a competition, the competition between Aeschylus and Euripides within the play may be seen as an *agon* within an *agon*. To the extent that the play succeeds in blurring the line which separates actors from audience and vice versa, it extends the dominion of art into the world beyond and willfully obscures for the moment recognition of Aristophanes' own artistic achievement. As long as the audience is eagerly engaged in weighing the merits of Aeschylus and Euripides as presented in the *Frogs*, it is ignoring the obvious ingenuity of their creator. Aeschylus and Euripides, the real artists, are dead, and Aristophanes knows that. Aeschylus in the play will be preferred over Euripides and will be led upward. But, like Eurydice, he will not see the light of real day again. No, Aristophanes, with the applause of the audience ringing in his ears, will this day carry home first prize.

The momentum of the play's spiral outward into the audience is balanced by the centripetal effect of a system of dynamic inner tensions. The *agon*, the contest between Aeschylus and Euripides which occupies most of the second half of the drama, is one hub of this inner motion; the *parodos*, the ritual procession of the underworld Chorus of Initiates which dominates the first half, is the other. Their countermotion sets up a 'field of force' powerful enough to contain the centrifugal tendencies of the comedy. The *agon*—even though there is consistent comic distortion throughout—is logical, analytical, forensic in procedure. It occurs in or near Pluto's palace, a court and seat of government where it is possible to conduct a fair hearing and reach a binding verdict. The trial itself seems open; evidence is presented for consideration by the public as well as by the official judge; the chorus comments regularly on the progress of the argumentation. During the *agon* we are shown conditions of rational investigation where the examination of evidence, arbitration, and negotiation are possible. Even though in the land of the dead and under a barrage of comic effects, we are in a world animated by the exercise of that discriminating critical intelligence which we consider one major aspect of our legacy from ancient Athens.

But the *parodos* exhibits equally characteristic and equally powerful aspects of 5th-century B.C. Athenian existence, too. These are what E. R. Dodds has called the "irrational," and William Arrowsmith the "turbulent," element in Greek experience. They find expression in a choral supplication of divinities of both the upper and lower world, in the lyric cry for torches to illuminate the shadowy pathway, in the throb of the dance, the tumescence of sexual response, the sound of flutes, and the aroma of burnt offerings. The *parodos* shapes these elements which derive from a dark mythic past, confining the orgiastic in the rhythms of ritual, and collecting for cult worship vivid personal emotions. In it the individual is submerged and needs no identity; the public, profane world has been exorcised, banished; ecstasy and communion—these are all.

The interplay of the attitudes and energies represented by and contained in the *agon* and the *parodos*, the *inter-play*—that is to say, their juxtaposition and manipulation through comic wit—this is the mode of the *Frogs*. It is surprise and recovery, mirror-mockery, idea compounding and counterpoising compounded idea; it is a ballet of plausibilities: in short, a very extravagant intellectual-artistic happening. It informs the limited and the local elements of the drama just as pervasively as the larger ones we have been discussing, and is the basis of the double characterization of Dionysus as god of both the public, critical realm of theater and of the mysteries which are conducted below. The chief symbols of the *Frogs* express well the sustained ambivalence of this brilliant tragi-comedy: the descent into the underworld, into the mysterious beyond, is a process which always needs attempting, and the scales of judgment offer always the possibility of proportionate understanding, of perspectives in perfect balance.

PART ONE

Interpretations

The Opening of the *Frogs*

by Leo Strauss

The *Frogs* is the only Aristophanean comedy at the beginning of which we see and hear a god. It is the only Aristophanean comedy the action of which proceeds from the design of a god. It differs from all plays hitherto discussed by the fact that it opens with a dialogue between a master and a slave. The master is Dionysos himself, the god of the theater. His slave Xanthias asks him whether he should say one of the things at which the spectators customarily laugh. Dionysos leaves him full freedom except that of using expressions that disgust Dionysos. His prohibition reminds us of the distinction between vulgar and Aristophanean comedy that we know from some of the parabaseis; Dionysos states the preference ordinarily stated by Aristophanes himself. After all, Aristophanes has been bred by Dionysos (*Clouds* 519). The *Frogs* is surely the only comedy that opens with the question, what should a character in the play do with a view to making the audience laugh? This means that the *Frogs* is the only comedy that does not simply open with a complaint or with moaning. Yet Xanthias is eager to make jokes because he wishes relief from the pain caused by the luggage that he is carrying, although he carries the burden while riding on a donkey, whereas his gentle master walks. Xanthias complains about the soreness of his shoulder. It is not necessary for our purpose to follow Dionysos, who wonders how Xanthias can be carrying something since he himself is carried, and, after this difficulty is disposed of, why since Xanthias denies that he derives any help from being carried by the donkey, he does not in his turn carry the donkey. Dionysos is a better arguer than Xanthias, just as he has a better taste than he; he deserves to be the master. It is more important for us to realize that in the beginning of the *Frogs* the complaint is not absent, but as it were subordinated to joking or laughter as the relief for complaint. Laughing presupposes suffering, while the reverse is not true. At any rate Dionysos, who at the beginning appears to be concerned with the right kind of comedy, soon proves to be concerned above all with the right kind of tragedy.

Dionysos commands Xanthias to get off the donkey, not in order to carry it, but because they have arrived at the god's first destination, the house of Herakles. Dionysos, clothed in a lion's skin and carrying a big club, knocks savagely at the door, which is opened by Herakles himself, who apparently has no servant; in contradistinction to Euripides and to Socrates in the corresponding scenes of the *Acharnians* and the *Clouds* respectively, he surely is not occupied. Contrary to Dionysos' expectation, which is not shared by Xanthias, Herakles is not frightened by his half brother's appearance but only incited by it to unquenchable laughter, for when dressing up for the role of Herakles, Dionysos had forgotten to take off his womanish garments. Dionysos obviously did not come to Herakles, as Dikaiopolis came to Euripides and as Euripides came to Agathon, in order to borrow a disguise; the god of the theater possesses all kinds of disguises. When Herakles asks him where on earth he has traveled in his ridiculous outfit, Dionysos replies that he has taken part in the naval battle of the Arginusai: a man or a god who lays claim to Heraklean prowess must have been able to do what many Athenian citizens and even slaves had done. His pretense to martial glory, as well as some other characteristics that he possesses, foreshadow Falstaff. The god of the theater is at the opposite pole from the fighter Herakles. Although the character responsible for the action of the *Frogs* is a god, he complies with Aristophanes' rule that characters who perform this function in his plays must be Athenian citizens. As he tells Herakles, while he was on a man-of-war on the way to the Arginusai or back, he read Euripides' *Andromeda,* and his heart became filled with an unsayably strong desire for the dead poet: no human being (and in particular not Herakles) can dissuade him from descending to Hades in order to bring Euripides back, for the poets who are still alive are bad. Herakles, for whose understanding Dionysos has a good-natured contempt, does not approve of his brother's liking for Euripides. He asks him why he does not try to bring back Sophocles from Hades rather than Euripides: the bringing back of Aeschylus is not even considered. Dionysos' decisive reason in favor of Euripides and against Sophocles is that one must be a scoundrel like Euripides in order to try to run away from the place where one belongs and, in particular, if one is dead, from Hades, but Sophocles was even-tempered (and hence content and just) here and is even-tempered (and hence content and just) there. Herakles draws Dionysos' attention to some other tragic poets;

among them is Agathon whom Dionysos, the admirer of Euripides, also admires, but even he is not comparable in his view to Euripides. According to Dionysos one can no longer find a naturally fertile poet who is able to utter risky expressions like "the foot of time," which Dionysos is crazy about and which Herakles rejects as altogether bad. One is tempted to think that Herakles, who cuts such a poor figure in the *Birds,* is sobriety itself when confronted with Dionysos' infatuation, just as Chairephon appeared to be on the side of law and order in the *Wasps* when confronted with the final madness of Philokleon. In Dionysos' view, Herakles, being concerned with nothing but food, understands nothing of poetry. He therefore turns to the purpose of his visit. Having decided to descend to Hades, he needs Herakles' guidance because he is wholly unfamiliar with Hades: there is no truth whatsoever in Heraclitus' saying that Dionysos and Hades are the same. Dionysos needs Herakles' guidance more particularly because of his softness or love of comfort; he wishes to know the most pleasant way down as well as about the hosts in Hades of whom the hero had made use when he had gone down to fetch Kerberos; he has provided himself with a lion's skin and a big club in order to be regarded and treated as Herakles while down there. His softness also explains why he needs the company of Xanthias; he needs quite a bit of luggage and hence a carrier of it. One wonders whether it is not his softness that underlies his love of Euripides. Herakles is shocked by his mad daring, but Dionysos' mind is made up; so great is his love of the theater that all his cowardice is powerless against it. While Herakles had gone down to Hades to fetch Kerberos because he was compelled to do so, Dionysos goes down to Hades in order to fetch Euripides because he loves Euripides' poetry. Dionysos refuses to consider any of the three kinds of suicide that Herakles proposes to him as ways to Hades, for he wishes to return. He is eager to learn from Herakles the way by which he had gone down, because Herakles has come back. Herakles gives him a gruesome description of the large and abysmally deep lake that one has to cross on Charon's tiny boat, of the innumerable snakes and other most terrible beasts, and the mass of foul mire and ever-flowing sewage in which the most unjust people (among them mother-beaters, but not Euripides) are thrown. Yet Dionysos is not afraid. Does he not believe in the terrors of Hades? He surely expects to find every kind of comfort on his journey. Although Herakles is reticent about the reception that he was given in Hades, he is truthful enough to add that Dionysos will see, after he has passed the terrors, in a most beautiful light like that of the sun, blessed groups of initiated men and women who will tell him everything he might need to know, for they dwell near the gates of Pluton. After having said this much,

Herakles bids Dionysos good-bye without making any further attempt
to dissuade him from his journey. He did not ask him why he wished
to look like Herakles in Hades. We suggest this explanation of this
strange wish. Dionysos does not wish to be recognized in order to be
able to see Euripides; he believes that he must steal Euripides just as
Herakles had stolen Kerberos, because he expects that the gods below
are anxious to keep the best poet; Herakles might be suspected of
anything, but surely not of stealing Euripides; the Heraklean appearance is the only one that can not possibly arouse in Hades the suspicion
that its wearer is after a poet.

Xanthias was of course excluded from the exchange between Dionysos and Herakles, but he did not accept that exclusion as a matter of
course. Three times he complained that no attention was paid to him;
after all, his shoulder still aches. He is accustomed to his master's paying attention to him; Dionysos is an easygoing, if not kind master,
who lives with his slave on a footing of equality. He accedes at once
to Xanthias' request that he leave him on earth and in his stead hire
as porter a corpse, which as such is on its way to Hades. Dionysos
sensibly refuses to pay the exorbitant sum demanded by the corpse,
which is just being carried out, and only then does the sensible Xanthias
declare that he is willing to carry the luggage to Hades. The relation
of Dionysos and Xanthias resembles that of friends, rather than that of
master and slave. Besides, not the terrors of Hades but the soreness
of his shoulder had induced Xanthias to consider allowing his master
to descend without him.

Dionysos and Xanthias arrive at the lake to be crossed on Charon's
boat. Charon does not allow Xanthias on his boat, since he is a slave
according to Athenian law, for he did not participate in the naval
battle, as he truthfully admits; unlike his master he does not lie. The
poor fellow is compelled to walk around the lake while carrying the
luggage; it looks as if the difference between free men and slaves will
be as important in Hades as it is on earth. At Charon's rude command
Dionysos must row, despite his complete lack of naval experience.
Charon comforts him by saying that the work will be made easy by
a song of the chorus of frogs, which they will soon hear. The frogs
sing of the beauty of the song that they chanted in honor of Dionysos
on the occasion of the Athenian festival dedicated to that son of Zeus.
They are not aware that the god is now listening to their singing;
they recognize Dionysos as little as Charon did, but unlike Charon
they are concerned with Dionysos. Dionysos loathes the frogs' music
but they continue with it, claiming to be beloved by the Muses, Pan,
and Apollon. While Dionysos' delicate ears suffer from the frogs'
croaking, his delicate hands suffer from the rowing. When the frogs

become aware of how much they annoy Dionysos, they annoy him on purpose. Thereupon Dionysos tries to silence them by outcroaking them, in which he succeeds. There is then a contest between the chorus and the individual responsible for the action of the play, a contest that ends with the victory of the "hero," as in the *Acharnians,* the *Wasps,* and the *Birds.* Yet in the *Frogs* the contest is not a contest through speech, nor does it occur in the center of the play. The conflict between the chorus and the hero in the *Frogs* is due merely to the failure of the chorus to recognize the hero. It is impossible to say whether that failure is caused by Dionysos' disguise. One may regard Dionysos' victory in the contest with the frogs as a good omen for his journey, but one must also say that we have only Dionysos' word for it that he defeated the frogs; the moment in which he claims to have defeated the frogs is the moment in which Charon's boat arrives at its destination, i.e., has left the region of the frogs.

When Dionysos and Xanthias meet on the far side of the lake, each claims to have seen the archcriminals of whom Herakles had spoken; but Dionysos at any rate had not given any sign of seeing them while he was rowing over the lake. He is surely uncertain now as to what they should do next. Xanthias suggests that they go on, since the place where they are, according to Herakles, is the region of the monstrous beasts. Yet, according to Herakles the place of the monstrous beasts is reached before the place of the archcriminals. Dionysos is now certain that Herakles has misinformed him about Hades, or more precisely that he has exaggerated the terrors of Hades in order both to frighten him (and thus to dissuade him from bringing back the hated Euripides) and to magnify his own descent to Hades. The only terror of Hades that Dionysos has experienced was the frogs, and those he overcame with ease. Entirely confident now, he is eager to meet a genuine monster of Hades. Xanthias obliges him by claiming to see the Empusa. Dionysos does not see it, either because it does not exist or because he is too frightened to see anything. He is so frightened that he urges his priest, who is sitting in the front row of the theater, to save him. He thus destroys the dramatic illusion without, however, becoming the spokesman for the poet (297; cf. 276). But the terror—the only terror of Hades that frightened Dionysos—passes soon. The god is free to wonder which god has been trying to ruin him. Xanthias tells him in effect that the god in question is Dionysos' desire for Euripides, or that Euripides is a danger to Dionysos. This suggestion remains ineffectual, for in this moment master and slave hear the playing of flutes and see flaming torches: they have left the region of the terrors and entered the region of the blessed initiated. They step aside in order to watch the procession of the initiated, i.e., of the main chorus of the play. The *Frogs* is the only play that has two choruses, not confronting each other (like the chorus of men and the chorus of women in the *Lysistrata*), but succeeding each other. The play is not called after the main chorus but after the chorus of the frogs, which is never heard of again after its brief contest with Dionysos. The duality of choruses corresponds to the duality of the terrors of Hades and the bliss in Hades. The chorus of frogs takes the place of a possible chorus of the archcriminals of Hades, i.e., of the admirers of Euripides (771-80), which would not have been bearable since it would have been a chorus, a *demos,* of archcriminals that professes the principles of injustice and is not converted by punishment after death. The title of the play draws our attention to this possible impossibility.

Stage and Action in the *Frogs*

by David Barrett

The dramatic performances at the Great Dionysian Festival, and probably also at the mid-winter festival of the Lenaea, took place in the Theatre of Dionysus, on the rocky southern slope of the Acropolis. The general shape of an ancient Greek theatre will be familiar to most readers: in Aristophanes' time, however, the audience was probably accommodated on wooden benches with earth foundations, and not on stone seats as in later theatres. There were seats for at least 10,000 spectators—the reference in the *Wasps* to 'countless tens of thousands' is clearly an exaggeration, but in the *Frogs* we hear of 'ten thousand men of sense' (literally 'ten thousand intelligences'), and *Plutus* contains a joke which seems to imply that the actual number was 13,000. At the foot of the semicircular terraced auditorium was the completely circular arena (known as the *orchestra*, or 'dance floor') where the Chorus performed, with the altar of Dionysus in the middle. Beyond this stood the stage building (*skene*), the exact design of which is still a matter of dispute. Most probably it was at this period a long wooden building containing dressing-rooms, etc., with a painted architectural facade on the auditorium side and one or more doors opening on to the stage. The existence of a raised stage for the actors in the fifth century was for a long time considered doubtful, but there are now signs of a return to the traditional view that a raised stage of some sort was used. It is thought that it probably consisted of a long but fairly narrow wooden platform, about four feet above the level of the *orchestra* and approachable from it by steps. There may also have been ramps or steps at the *ends* of the stage, leading down to the *parodos*—the passage between the stage building and the extreme ends of the rows of seats, providing access to the theatre from outside and leading directly into the *orchestra*. Part of the stage building must have been on two storeys, so that the painted facade could have

a window on the upper floor and thus represent a two-storeyed house:
for the rest of its length the building seems to have had a single storey
with a flat roof, thus providing an upper stage for which both tragic
and comic playwrights found a great variety of uses. In the *Wasps* the
skene would thus have represented exactly what it actually was: a two-
storeyed building with a single-storeyed extension; and we can see
from this play that the upper level could be reached in two ways—
by going up a ladder or a flight of steps leading directly from the stage
to the flat-roofed section, or by entering the 'house' by the door and
'going upstairs' inside, so as to appear at an upper window. Actors
could make their entrances and exits either by the door or doors in
the facade or by the *parodos,* in which case they then had to mount
to the stage from *orchestra* level. The actors seem to have been quite
free to perform in the *orchestra* as well as on the stage, and, in comedy
at least, it looks as if the Chorus could make occasional incursions
onto the stage, as appears to happen in the 'battle' scene of the *Wasps.*

The Theatre of Dionysus was equipped with two pieces of stage
machinery, devised no doubt to serve the needs of tragedy, but often
exploited in the comedies. The first was a device known as the *eccyclema,* enabling scenes to be set behind the visible facade and then
'rolled out' (it is not clear how) on to the stage. It was probably a
fairly simple device, such as a large concealed door in the facade with
a wooden floor attached behind it: such a door would be hinged at
one side, with a wheel or castor at the other so that it could be pushed
open easily. (Agathon, in *The Poet and the Women,* has to call for a
slave to push him back again.) Another possibility is that the *eccyclema*
was on the upper level and was simply pushed out of the 'upper room'
on to the flat roof. The second device, known simply as 'the machine,'
enabled gods and goddesses to make spectacular descents from heaven,
as they frequently had to do at the end of a tragedy in order to sort
out the mess the characters had got themselves into. Euripides made
extensive use of it: at the end of *Medea,* for example, the protagonist
and her dead children are wafted away in a chariot drawn by dragons.
In *The Poet and the Women* he is given a taste of his own medicine.

II

Assuming the stage arrangements to have been roughly as I have
described them (though it must be repeated that many details are
matters of conjecture), it is interesting to work out the way in which
some of the scenes in the comedies must have been staged, and see
how Aristophanes exploited his resources. Often there are cues in the

text to help us. Let us take a look, for example, at the opening scenes of the *Frogs*.

Dionysus, puffing and panting, and Xanthias, on his human donkey, enter the *orchestra* by the *parodos*, passing close to a section of the audience, whom Xanthias surveys with disgust. As they mount the steps to the stage, and the conversation turns upon burdens, attention is called to the plight of the 'donkey': 'you'd better change places with him,' Dionysus suggests. At last they reach the stage proper, and the door of Heracles' house. ('You see, I've walked the whole way.') Dionysus and Heracles converse, while Xanthias and his mount provide comic business in the background. Eventually the donkey wanders off, via the *parodos*, and re-enters the stage building from the rear. Heracles says good-bye to Dionysus, whips off his mask and lion-skin, lies down on a stretcher, and is carried out of another door as the Corpse. (The ex-donkey is now one of the bearers.) After being intercepted by Dionysus, the Corpse is carried down the steps (this would suggest a descent to the underworld) and out by the *parodos*. As soon as he is out of sight, the Corpse nips through the back door into the dressing-room, and a moment later returns as Charon, poling his comical boat-on-wheels along the *parodos* towards the *orchestra*. Dionysus and Xanthias, who have had to carry out a bit of business with the luggage to give time for all this, now start their downward journey. By this time Charon, already visible to most of the audience, is just rounding the corner of the stage: Dionysus and Xanthias see the prow of the boat before Charon himself comes into view. They descend to the 'shore': Dionysus gets into the boat, but Xanthias is told that he will have to walk right round the 'lake,' i.e., the *orchestra*. This he does, probably by a roundabout route, frequently losing his way among the gangways of the auditorium. Meanwhile the boat is launched, and Dionysus rows right out into the 'open waters' of the *orchestra*. The Frogs now enter, leaping and hopping, by the *parodos* (greeted, perhaps, by a cheer from the audience, who think they are the real Chorus: after all, the title of the play has been announced as the *Frogs*). They dance around the boat, singing and croaking in chorus, until Dionysus succeeds in driving them away. By this time he has rowed right across to the side of the *orchestra* farthest from the stage, and he lands at the feet of his own priest in the center of the front row of seats. Charon rows rapidly away, and Xanthias rejoins his master. But now the Empusa appears, a fearsome monster which keeps changing its shape: perhaps some of the frog-dancers again, in horrific masks, peeping out in turn from under a blanket. Dionysus, in terror, clutches the skirts of his priest, and then flees up the central gangway, to the delight of the audience.

But Xanthias succeeds in exorcising the apparition. They start back towards the stage, but now the real Chorus enters, and they are obliged to crouch down at the edge of the *orchestra,* where they remain until they decide to join in the dancing themselves. The dance brings them back to the foot of the stage steps, and when Dionysus inquires the way to the palace, the Chorus reply, 'It's just behind you now'—and so, by Pluto, it is. They have reached their journey's end. Xanthias retrieves the luggage, and Dionysus mounts the steps towards the palace door. Meanwhile the women dancers, who are not going to be needed again (they too, perhaps, are played by the boys of the Frog Chorus), are given their cue to leave the *orchestra:* 'And I,' runs the text, implying a fresh speaker, 'will go with the girls and women.' The men remain to dance in the meadow of roses and sing of the Mysteries, while Dionysus plucks up courage to knock at the door.

The Dionysus of the *Frogs:*

A Comment on the *Dioniso* of Carlo Pascal

by Étienne Lapalus

Dionysus is the protagonist of the *Frogs;* he is also the figure most strongly parodied, the one that comic portraiture turns into veritable caricature. Why has Aristophanes chosen this god as the principal character of his play, why does he make him judge of the tournament he sets up between Aeschylus and Euripides in Hades? Why has he represented him elsewhere as a pitiful creature, as a character so burlesqued?

Actually, Dionysus, the god of the theater, has a perfectly natural place in the literary debate between two dramatic posts as judge of that debate. But his godlike character, which justifies his appearance in the drama, seems from time to time to have been forgotten by Aristophanes. In any case it is not the god of the theater Aristophanes is ridiculing. But one can ask, however, if the Dionysus who in the first part of the play is involved in the frolics of the chorus of the Eleusinian mysteries could not in fact be the god worshipped at Eleusis along with Demeter and Kore? Carlo Pascal in *Dioniso,* his study "of religion and religious parody in Aristophanes" (Catane, Battiato, 1911), raised once again this familiar question and reached conclusions which can be summed up concisely: *In the* Frogs *Aristophanes has stripped Dionysus of all his divine attributes; he has made him a vulgar and ridiculous man, a brash trickster who is present like a stranger at the rites celebrated before him.*

In the *Frogs* Dionysus is not a god, and in particular he is not the god of Eleusis: these are the essential points of Pascal's thesis, which he argues very circumspectly. He admits that the first part of the play shows the descent of the 'god' into Hades. But mythology did in fact attribute such an exploit to Dionysus who was at Eleusis thought to

"The Dionysus of the Frogs." *Excerpted from "Le Dionysus et l'Héraclès des Grenouilles,"* Revue des Études Grecques, *XLVII (1934), 1-20. Copyright 1934 by* Revue des Études Grecques. *Reprinted, in a slightly abridged form without notes, by permission of the publisher. Translated by Nancy Ann Trease.*

be a chthonic deity. If we did not already know this, several verses of the *Frogs* would tell us. Lines 215ff. allude to the feast of Χύτροι [on which wine-jars—χύτροι—were sealed and the dead propitiated] which is celebrated on the third day of Anthesteria in honor of Chthonian Dionysus. But Carlo Pascal says in effect that Aristophanes seems never to have dreamed of the real descent of Dionysus into Hades: he has attired Dionysus in Heracles' clothes and made of the god a human being foolish and low for the purpose of parodying one of the Labors of Heracles. Any consideration of the moral character of Dionysus in the *Frogs*, he argues, leads to the conclusion that he cannot be a god.

From the first scene Dionysus does show himself to be a ridiculous buffoon, and at the beginning of the play one might suppose he was watching a clown's entrance into a modern circus ring. He engages in jokes, in word play that Xanthias understands not at all; he introduces himself to the audience under a grotesque name—Διόνυσος υἱὸς Σταμνίου (Dionysus, son of the Wine-Jar [22])—and the manner of his arrival at the house of Heracles is as exaggerated as that of a puppet-show. He is a coward. He is overwhelmed by foolish terror when confronted with all the things Heracles had described, and this terror manifests itself in a purely physical form (cf. 307-8; see also 479ff.). In order to intimidate the underworld divinities he assumes the name of Her-acles-the-Brave. When the hostesses of Hades' wayside inn threaten to thrash the person they imagine to be Heracles, Dionysus puts on the garments of his slave, then hurries to regain his own when he notices the smell of a good meal and sees a pretty dancer (549ff.). Chastity and sobriety are not his greatest virtues. Xanthias says of his master (739-40):

> Πῶς γὰρ οὐχὶ γεννάδας
> ὅστις γε πίνειν οἶδε καὶ βινεῖν μόνον;

Well-born! I'll say!—his only passions are wining and wenching.

and Euripides greets the god—or pseudo-god—with this title (1472):

> ὦ μιαρώτατ' ἀνθρώπων

O most wretched man.

In any event we would doubt Dionysus was a reputable person: if nothing else, his conversation with Heracles had convinced us of that. This, then, constitutes our broad understanding of the character of Dionysus: he is a coarse and lazy trickster, a man vulgar and sensual, all in all a being who about him nothing of the divine.

If the moral character of this person prohibits our seeing him as a god, his surprise and his attitude during the mystic ceremonies at

which he is present especially prevent any consideration of him as
the divinity worshipped at Eleusis. According to Carlo Pascal, it would
be very strange for Chthonian Dionysus of Eleusis, a god of the underworld, to come to Heracles to ask the route to Hades, and his astonishment when Heracles tells him that there he will encounter the
Initiates of Eleusis would be impossible to explain.

—The sound of flutes will surround you—Heracles told him—;
you'll see a beautiful light, like sunlight here, myrtle forests, happy
throngs of men and women, and a lively clapping of hands.
—And these—asks Dionysus—who are they?
—The Initiates.   (154-58)

But when the chorus of initiates actually appears, Dionysus, who
cannot even remember Heracles' description, stops in surprise like a
curious spectator (321-22):

'Ησυχίαν τοίνυν ἄγειν
βέλτιστόν ἐστιν, ὡς ἂν εἰδῶμεν σαφῶς.

Let's keep quiet until we know what's happening.

And with two exceptions he keeps quiet throughout the ceremony;
his interjections are the clownish jokes of a man who obviously does
not understand the spectacle he beholds.

Thus, once again to summarize Pascal's views, nothing permits us
to identify the Dionysus of the *Frogs* with the god of Eleusis: *Aristophanes' Dionysus is a human being, and it is because of his hostility
toward the Dionysian rites that the poet has lowered this god to the
rank of a vulgar mortal.*

Carlo Pascal's analysis of Dionysus' character unquestionably is of
value; everything that is vulgar, grotesque and even odious in the god's
character has been well analyzed by him. But should one conclude
from the real baseness of Dionysus in this comedy that he is a man
and not a god? Mr. Pascal argues that it is because of antipathy towards
the Dionysian cult that Aristophanes has stripped the god of his
divinity. For my part, I believe the poet has attempted to brighten
the play at the expense of Dionysus as an Eleusinian divinity.

Eleusis and its mysteries supply the invisible decor, the distant
perspectives of the *Frogs*. Too often this play has been considered to
be poorly constructed, made up of two parts in juxtaposition treating
entirely different subjects. Too often the only feature noticed has been
the literary debate between Aeschylus and Euripides that forms the
second part of the play. In my opinion Dionysus' descent into Hades
and the representation in caricature of an aspect of the Eleusinian

ceremonies are not merely *hors d'oeuvres*—and the play itself, in its entirety, does not seem incoherent to me. It is precisely the scene where the initiates appear that dominates the play, not only because of its historical interest but because of its place in the structure of the drama.

The historical interest has been summed up concisely by Willems in a note to line 316 of his translation of the play:

> Here begins an episode that circumstances made particularly interesting to the spectators. The place of the celebration of the Mysteries in the religious life of Athenians is well known. Since the Spartan occupation of Decelea in 413 the solemn procession which each year in September wound its way to Eleusis had not taken place. One time only in these eight years, in 408, thanks to measures taken by Alcibiades, had it been carried out with the customary pomp. Now that it is prohibited on earth, the poet has it occur in Hades.

Thus the representation of the Eleusinian mysteries in the *Frogs* has—in a serious sense—a religious value. Also, it unifies the play in a manner which is not apparent at first. By arousing nostalgia in the Athenians, it makes them favorably disposed toward the man who allowed them in 408 to go solemnly to Eleusis as before. Therefore when Aristophanes, speaking in the voice of the chorus in the parabasis, gives useful counsel to the city about employing in times of duress its best and most able men, he can expect that it will turn to Alcibiades as the only one who, despite his faults, could redeem the situation. Further, the evocation of Eleusis and its mysteries prepares the denouement. Dionysus, having instituted a contest between Aeschylus and Euripides, will carry the victor, Aeschylus, back to earth. Aeschylus is the poet of religion and it is interesting to note that Aristophanes identifies him with the mysteries several times. At the outset of the contest proper Aeschylus invokes Demeter, the great goddess of Eleusis, praying that he may be worthy of her mystic rites (887). In addressing him (851), Dionysus applies to Aeschylus the sacred epithet of mystic divinity, πολυτίμητος—highly-honored. Finally, Aeschylus for a while maintains mystic silence (832ff.). In itself and in its evocative power the Eleusinian scene is of central significance in the *Frogs*.

There are several reasons for believing Dionysus himself is not out of place in this Eleusinian frame of reference and for seeing in him the divine personage associated with the cult worship of Eleusis. For Carlo Pascal, Dionysus of Eleusis is no more than a god of two aspects, at the same time sovereign of the dead and divinity of vegetation, who as such receives double homage at the feast of Haloa and at the Anthesteria. And in truth there are in the *Frogs* no allusions to these aspects of Dionysus. But Dionysus appeared also at Eleusis as a mystic initiate, as one of the great heroes of legend who first experienced the benefits of initiation and can therefore guarantee its value in the eyes of simple men. Mythology, as we have seen, attributed to Dionysus a descent into Hades. It is useful to remember the role of the descent to the underworld in the mystery religions and the failure to which audacious attempts are condemned when the hero who undertakes them has failed to undergo preliminary initiation. We know of the initiation of Dionysus, an initiation the legend of Halimont had irreverently transposed into a carnal union of the god with a certain Proshymnos. There should therefore be no reason for surprise if Dionysus—initiated before his descent into Hades and returned successfully from that enterprise—should by some be associated with the cult of Eleusis and if the memory of his first initiation should be preserved in certain rather strange rites perhaps involving sacred relics. It is this Dionysus, the mystic initiate who is associated with the divinities of Eleusis, that I believe I recognize in the Dionysus of the *Frogs.*

The buffoonery and sensuality of his character, which prevent Carlo Pascal from seeing in him a god, do not in reality interfere with my identification. The Dionysus of Eleusis is a facetious god, fond of good living, as is well indicated by the Eleusinian inscription where he is called παραπαίζων, that is to say, "one who loves to play, who loves and understands pleasantry." As to his sensuality and other faults of character, they correspond well with certain myths of Dionysus the mystic initiate, and verses 48-60 of the *Frogs* seem to contain an allusion to one of them. When Dionysus arrives at the house of Heracles, the hero asks the god, "Where are you going?" and Dionysus replies with a play on words, Ἐπεβάτευον Κλεισθένει ("I was aboard the Kleisthenes") (48). Carlo Pascal explains this as an allusion to a homosexual relationship between Dionysus and Kleisthenes, and he has no trouble showing that the masculine loves of the god were well known and that Aristophanes did not pass up any opportunity for commenting in his comedies on the vices of Kleisthenes. But the allusion made at the moment of Dionysus' arrival at the house of Heracles to ask him the route to Hades can be seen to have a more precise meaning.

When Dionysus was searching for the route to Hades, he searched in vain until he encountered Proshymnos and asked for information. Proshymnos possessed the information Dionysus wanted and was willing to give it, but not, as the legend goes, "without reward." We know that this adventure was the subject of a "sacred story" enacted at the Lesser Mysteries of Agra that were celebrated in honor of Dionysus in the month Anthesteria. The union of Dionysus and Proshymnos had the significance and effect of a mystic initiation because it had been the condition and guarantee of a happy voyage to the land of the dead. It is certainly the Chthonian Dionysus, initiated in the mysteries of Eleusis, who is the hero of this adventure. Therefore it is impossible not to recall this story when hearing Dionysus' equivocal response to Heracles. Aristophanes knew this legend; he knew also the strange rites—unexplained for a long time—that preserved at Eleusis the memory of this first initiation of the god. It is not unintentional that Dionysus alludes to his vice at the moment when he comes to ask Heracles the road to the underworld, that is to say, at the moment when he comes to be initiated a second time.

But while this "second initiation" of Dionysus recalls his first, and may in some respects be analogous to that which the faithful might undergo at Eleusis, it is at the same time an initiation in caricature in which Aristophanes pokes fun at the goals and the means of Eleusinian ceremonies and at the sentiments expressed by initiates at moments of religious exaltation. "Happy is the one among men dwelling on the earth who has seen these things; he who has not experienced the sacred rites, and he who has taken part, after death will not have the same lot in the realm of the shades." Thus the *Hymn to Demeter* expresses the goal of initiation and the happiness reserved in the other world for initiates only. Pindar, Sophocles, Plato, and Socrates would not express it differently; they are all in agreement in affirming the grandeur of the goal of initiation. But certain characters in the comedies of Aristophanes have lost all sense of this grandeur. Trygaeus in *Peace* cannot see initiation as anything except a formality to be accomplished as assurance of a comfortable life in Hades. At the moment he tries to free Peace, who has been emprisoned in a deep cavern, Hermes intervenes and reminds him that Zeus has decreed death for whoever should be discovered attempting to disinter her. In annoyance Trygaeus responds, "O all right! Lend me three drachmas so I can buy a pig and get initiated" (*Peace,* 374-75). Trygaeus is evidently a practical man who thinks that once he is dead it will be too late to have himself initiated. Dionysus comes to be initiated by Heracles because he is compelled to descend into Hades and wishes to assure himself an agreeable journey. He seeks in initiation a means of continuing while on his trip the joyous life he leads on earth. Dionysus assumes that when Heracles went to Hades he managed to find comfortable accommodations, so he asks direction to the houses of prostitution. Initiation obviously has no religious value for either of them. To be initiated is to gain a guide to Hades, with numerous details about hotels and places of pleasure. Heracles in his own way ridicules the goal of initiation because before he gives Dionysus the information he requests, he suggests to him a number of ways to kill oneself and therefore to arrive in Hades with certainty. Initiation—so Heracles seems to think—

merely provides men a means to the kingdom of Shades; for this there
is no need to go to Eleusis: it is sufficient simply to kill oneself in any
manner.

The religious enthusiasm experienced by mystics at the decisive
moment of initiation has also in my opinion been mocked in the
Frogs. It is useful in pursuing this line of thought to recall the celebrated passage of Plutarch where the author describes the feelings of
the Eleusinian initiate during the course of the ceremonies:

> The Soul, at the moment of death, experiences the same feeling as those
> who are initiated into the Greater Mysteries. . . . There are at first haz-
> ardous courses, painful detours, disquieting marches among the shadows.
> Then, just before the end the terror is at its zenith, the shivering, the trem-
> bling, the cold sweat, the horror. But then a marvelous light breaks upon
> the eyes; one passes through holy places and plains where voices and
> dances are heard; sacred words and divine apparitions inspire a religious
> reverence. Then man, from that time perfect and initiated, having become
> free and without constraint, celebrates the mysteries, a crown upon his
> head. He lives among men holy and pure . . . .

There is no doubt that the descent of Dionysus into the underworld
in the *Frogs* is a caricature of the kind of experience later recorded by
Plutarch; it is clearly a parody of the sentiments recorded there. The
"disquieting marches" we find in lines 277 and following: Dionysus
and Xanthias arrive in the land of monsters, the god is afraid and hides
behind his slave. As soon as Xanthias announces a danger, Dionysus
shivers, trembles in horror, and becomes pale. It is not until the end
of this journey through fear that our travellers reach the Eleusinian
plains where the joyful Iacchos, surrounded by dancers and song, conducts the procession of those who have been initiated.

My conclusion therefore is: *Dionysus, introduced into the* Frogs *as
god of the theater, has actually been chosen by Aristophanes as the
hero of the play because the poet by evoking the memory of Dionysus'
mystic initiation was able to caricature many aspects of the Eleusinian
mysteries.*

The Eleusinian Mysteries

by George E. Mylonas

What we can learn about the Eleusinian Mysteries is certainly very limited. We know of certain rites that were not, however, part of the secret celebration; we can figure out certain acts that were part of the Mysteries, such as the enactment of the sacred pageant; we know nothing of the substance of the Mysteries, of the meaning derived even from the sacred drama which was performed. Explanations suggested by scholars thus far, and philosophic conceptions and parallels, are based upon assumptions and the wish to establish the basis on which the Mysteries rested. These accounts do not seem to correspond to the facts. The secret of the Mysteries *was kept a secret* successfully and we shall perhaps never be able to fathom it or unravel it.

For years, since my early youth, I have tried to find out what the facts were. Hope against hope was spent against the lack of monumental evidence; the belief that inscriptions would be found on which the Hierophants had recorded their ritual and its meaning has faded completely; the discovery of a subterranean room filled with the archives of the cult, which dominated my being in my days of youth, is proved an unattainable dream since neither subterranean rooms nor archives for the cult exist at Eleusis; the last Hierophant carried with him to the grave the secrets which had been transmitted orally for untold generations, from the one high priest to the next. A thick, impenetrable veil indeed still covers securely the rites of Demeter and protects them from the curious eyes of modern students. How many nights and days have been spent over books, inscriptions, and works of art by eminent scholars in their effort to lift the veil! How many wild and ingenious theories have been advanced in superhuman effort to explain the Mysteries! How many nights I have spent standing on the steps of the Telesterion, flooded with the magic silver light of a Mediterranean moon, hoping to catch the mood of the initiates, hoping that the human soul might get a glimpse of what the rational mind could not investigate! All in vain—the ancient world has kept its secret well and the Mysteries of Eleusis remain unrevealed.

The few details that we know are inadequate to give us a complete understanding of the substance of the rites. What do we know about those rites? We know that different degrees of initiation existed, the most advanced of which was known as the *epopteia*. We know that all people of Hellenic speech and untainted by human blood, with the exception of barbarians, were eligible to be initiated into the Mysteries—men, women, children, and even slaves. We know that the main initiation, the *telete,* included at least three elements: the *dromena,* the things which were enacted; the *deiknymena,* the things which were shown; and the *legomena,* the words which were spoken. The spoken words and the sacred objects revealed by the Hierophant remain unknown. We may assume that the pageant of the wanderings of Demeter, the story of Persephone, and the reunion of mother and daughter formed part of the *dromena;* that it was a passion play which aimed not only to unfold the myth of the Goddesses to the initiates but also to make these initiates partake of the experiences of the Goddesses, to share with them the distress, the travail, the exultation, and the joy which attended the loss of Persephone and her reunion with the mother. Certainly the story of the *Mater Dolorosa* of antiquity contains elements that appeal to the human heart and imagination. "With burning torches Persephone is sought, and when she is found the rite is closed with general thanksgiving and a waving of torches." We may assume that the fortunes of Demeter and Persephone symbolized the vegetation cycle—life, death, and life again: "the sprouting of the new crop is a symbol of the eternity of life"; that they gave the initiates confidence to face death and a promise of bliss in the dark domain of Hades whose rulers became their protectors and friends through initiation. But can we go beyond this point and imagine more fully the substance of the Mysteries?

There are a good many scholars who believe that there was no more to the Mysteries than the few facts and surmises we have summarized; there are others who believe that their substance was so simple that it escapes us just because of its simplicity. There are even a few who maintain that the secret was kept because actually there was no secret worth keeping. The testimonies of the ancient world would prove untenable the suggestion of the agnostics. I believe that nearer the mark are the scholars who are trying to suggest a meaning which could have appeal to so many people for so long. Of the variety of suggestions made we shall quote but three because they seem to us that they take us as far towards a solution of the mystery as we can hope to go with the available evidence.

Nilsson suggests that the Mysteries based "on the foundation of the old agrarian cult a hope of immortality and a belief in the eternity of life, not for the individual but for the generations which spring one from another. Thus, also, there was developed on the same foundation a morality of peace and good will, which strove to embrace humanity in a brotherhood without respect to state allegiance and civil standing. The hope and the belief and the morality were those of the end of the archaic age." [1]

Guthrie has suggested that the Eleusinian cult was based upon the Homeric (and I would add also Mycenaean) conception of the hereafter, and of an existence after death somewhat altered to benefit the initiates.[2] "In Homer," he states, voicing the generally accepted ideas, "dead exist indeed, but they are strengthless, witless wraiths, uttering thin bodiless shrieks as they flit to and fro in the shadowy house of Hades." And we may recall in this regard Achilles' words, "I should choose, so I might live on earth, to serve as the hireling of another, of some portionless man whose livelihood was but small, rather than to be lord over all the dead that have perished," whom he described as "the unheeding dead, the phantoms of men outworn." [3] But Homer also has an Elysium, a very pleasant place indeed, to which went special people for special reasons; Menelaos was destined to go there because he "had Helen as his wife and in the eyes of the Gods he was the son-in-law of Zeus." Guthrie suggests that perhaps this Elysium was promised to the initiates of the Eleusinian cult, and that promise of course filled them with bliss and joy. The suggestion seems plausible, especially since its inception could go back to the Mycenaean age when the Mysteries were established at Eleusis. It holds no punishment for the uninitiated and only the promise of good things for the *mystai;* the two correspond to the prospects held out by the Hymn. It is simple, but does not seem to have any relation to the Goddesses of Eleusis, whose role was not that of assigning dead to different categories.

"Are we left quite in the dark as to the secret of salvation that Eleusis cherished and imported?" asks Farnell, and we may well join him in his answer. "When we have weighed all the evidence and remember the extraordinary fascination a spectacle exercised upon the Greek temperament, the solution of the problem is not so remote or so perplexing. The solemn fast and preparation, the mystic food eaten and drunk, the moving passion-play, the extreme sanctity of the ἱερά (sacred relics) revealed, all these influences could induce in the wor-

[1] M. P. Nilsson, *Greek Popular Religion,* p. 63.

[2] W. K. C. Guthrie, *Orpheus and the Greek Religion,* p. 149.

[3] *Odyssey,* 11, vv. 476 and 489-91.

shipper, not indeed the sense of absolute union with the divine nature such as the Christian sacrament . . . but at least the feeling of intimacy and friendship with the deities, and a strong current of sympathy was established by the mystic contact." Since those deities ruled over the lower world, people would feel that "those who won their friendship by initiation in this life would by the simple logic of faith regard themselves as certain to win blessings at their hands in the next. And this," suggests Farnell, "as far as we can discern, was the ground on which flourished the Eleusinian hope." [4]

Was this conception sufficient to justify the enthusiasm of the ancient world? What was the role and significance of Demeter who was the major deity of the Mysteries and who was not the mistress of the lower world? Plouton the master of that world had from all appearances a very secondary role and Persephone would emerge as the dominant power if the suggestion is accepted. Both Farnell and Guthrie reason well what can be obtained from the available evidence, and give us perhaps a portion of the significance of the Mysteries. I agree with them since I had reached similar conclusions; but I cannot help feeling that there is much more to the cult of Eleusis that has remained a secret; that there is meaning and significance that escapes us.

Whatever the substance and meaning of the Mysteries was, the fact remains that the cult of Eleusis satisfied the most sincere yearnings and the deepest longings of the human heart. The initiates returned from their pilgrimage to Eleusis full of joy and happiness, with the fear of death diminished and the strengthened hope of a better life in the world of shadows: "Thrice happy are those of mortals, who having seen those rites depart for Hades; for to them alone is it granted to have true life there; to the rest all there is evil," Sophokles cries out exultantly. And to this Pindar with equal exultation answers: "Happy is he who, having seen these rites goes below the hollow earth; for he knows the end of life and he knows its god-sent beginning." [5] When we read these and other similar statements written by the great or nearly great of the ancient world, by the dramatists and the thinkers, when we picture the magnificent buildings and monuments constructed at Eleusis by great political figures like Peisistratos, Kimon, Perikles, Hadrian, Marcus Aurelius and others, we cannot help but believe that the Mysteries of Eleusis were not an empty, childish affair devised by shrewd priests to fool the peasant and the ignorant, but a philosophy of life that possessed substance and meaning and imparted a modicum of truth to the yearning human soul. That belief is strengthened when

---

[4] L. R. Farnell, *The Cults of the Greek States*, III, p. 197.
[5] Sophokles, *Fragm.*, 719 (Dindorf). Pindar, *Fragm.*, 102 (Oxford).

we read in Cicero that Athens has given nothing to the world more excellent or divine than the Eleusinian Mysteries.[6]

Let us recall again that the rites of Eleusis were held for some two thousand years; that for two thousand years civilized humanity was sustained and ennobled by those rites. Then we shall be able to appreciate the meaning and importance of Eleusis and of the cult of Demeter in the pre-Christian era. When Christianity conquered the Mediterranean world, the rites of Demeter, having perhaps fulfilled their mission to humanity, came to an end. The "bubbling spring" of hope and inspiration that once existed by the Kallichoron well became dry and the world turned to other living sources for sustenance. The cult that inspired the world for so long was gradually forgotten, and its secrets were buried with its last Hierophant.

[6] Cicero, *De Legibus*, 2, 14, 36.

The Parodos in Aristophanes' *Frogs*

by M. Tierney

It has been almost universally assumed that the Chorus in the Parodos of the *Frogs* represents the initiates of the Eleusinian Mysteries assembled in Hades, and performing in the happy Other-world the same joyous rites that were performed at Athens in the great procession to Eleusis during the autumn festival of Demeter and Kore. This is undoubtedly the interpretation of the Scholiasts, and except for certain differences in matters of detail, it has been accepted in general by modern scholars.

The grounds for this interpretation are plain enough. In the first place, it was natural in late antiquity, when the materials upon which our commentaries rest were put together, to refer all mention anywhere in Greek literature of mystic rites to the most celebrated of mysteries—those of Eleusis. In the second place, the superficial indications supplied by the poem itself readily suggest an Eleusinian model. The most obvious of these indications is the predominant place given to Iacchos. Though early identified with Dionysos, this divinity seems to have had an Eleusinian origin (Herodotus viii, 65), and the principal public ceremony at the Greater Eleusinia in Boedromion was perhaps the imposing procession, in which, as Herodotus suggests, as many as thirty thousand people took part, when his image was borne amid shouts and songs along the Sacred Way from his shrine in Athens to Eleusis. The Parodos seems at first sight to present us with a half-serious, half-comic reproduction of this procession, as the poet imagines it enacted by the dead initiates in Hades. We have the joyful songs to Iacchos wherewith it begins, the πρόρρησις (354-71) or proclamation in which the δᾳδοῦχος (a *torch-bearer* at the festival of Eleusinian Demeter, whose torch represented her as searching for her daughter Persephone) warns off all those not permitted to participate in the rites, a song to Demeter, the chief Eleusinian divinity, and a passage

"*The Parodos in Aristophanes'* Frogs" by M. Tierney. From Proceedings of the Royal Irish Academy, XLII, Section C (*1935*), 199-202. Copyright *1935* by the Royal Irish Academy. Reprinted, without notes and with the addition in parentheses of translations of some Greek terms, by permission of the Royal Irish Academy.

in which various Athenian celebrities are reviled after a fashion that seems to recall the γεφυρισμός, or ritual abuse of those taking part in the journey to Eleusis.

A very slight examination, however, suffices to show that these analogies, at first sight so striking, are after all no more than superficial. To begin with, the importance assigned in the Parodos to Iacchos seems rather disproportionate. Altogether four hymns in his honor are included in it, while Demeter herself gets only one, and that a brief one (384-93). More surprising than this is the fact that Kore-Persephone, who was only slightly less important at Eleusis than her mother Demeter, and far more important than Iacchos, gets none at all. A curious blindness, no doubt induced by the plausibility of the ancient interpretation, seems to have deceived all scholars hitherto into thinking that she does; but for such a hymn, addressed directly to Kore by any title, the Parodos will be searched in vain. It may be argued that the procession was peculiarly sacred to Iacchos, as his image was carried in it; but we know that certain ἱερά (sacred relics) were also carried, and these ἱερά must have had to do with the two goddesses. It seems incredible that Iacchos should have so completely put them in the background as is apparently the case here.

A second difficulty is provided by the so-called πρόρρησις (354-71). In the Eleusinian Mysteries this proclamation was made in Athens in the Stoa Poikile on the fifteenth Boedromion, four days before the procession, and was directed against barbarians and murderers. In the Parodos, assuming that the Eleusinian explanation is the true one, the πρόρρησις is made after the procession has started. The procession itself seems to take place at night, whereas that to Eleusis was by day. The πρόρρησις has nothing to say about barbarians or murderers, but warns off three classes of people: (1) those who are unacquainted with certain λόγοι (liturgical formulae), are impure in heart, have no knowledge of the Muses' orgies, or have not been initiated in the Bacchic rites of Cratinus the Bull-Eater; (2) those who have committed acts of treachery against the State during war; and finally (3) those who have offended the poet and his chorus or have resented attacks made on themselves in the ancestral rites of Dionysos. Neither in the place nor in the objects of this warning is there anything in the smallest degree connected with Eleusis.

A third difficulty arises in regard to the σκώμματα (gibes) contained in lines 416-30 of the Parodos, which are usually equated with the Eleusinian γεφυρισμοί (rites at the bridge). From what little we know about these latter, it appears that as the procession passed over the river Kephisos just outside Athens, those leading it were the object of abuse from a man or men seated on the bridge. In the Parodos,

on the other hand, the reviling is done by the processionists themselves, and is directed against certain well-known people outside their
ranks—in other words, the situation is exactly the opposite to what
took place at the Eleusinia.

These are difficulties internal to the Parodos itself. Other and more
serious difficulties of an external character have long since been remarked. In 1858, Gerhard pointed out the great improbability that
any poet would have dared in the year 405 to depict, even distantly,
under a humorous aspect, a procession which had for eight years been
suspended owing to the presence of an enemy force in Attica. The one
exception to this suspension had been the year 407, when the procession was rendered possible by Alcibiades. That Aristophanes could
have been referring to this one exception is highly unlikely in view of
the fact that at the time of the play Alcibiades was once again un-
popular and in exile, and his exploit a bitter memory. This difficulty
seems to me almost insuperable. It is at any rate more serious than
another often put forward, to the effect that parodies of the Eleusinian
rites were, as is well known, visited with the severest penalties. We
cannot be certain that every kind of parody was punished; it may be
that what was forbidden was either the sacrilegious performance of the
final rites of initiation, as in the famous case of Andocides, or the
revelation of certain very sacred formularies or rubrics, as in the more
doubtful case of Aeschylus. The serious thing was probably not the
parody or revelation of beliefs involved in the Eleusinian rites, but
that of the rites themselves. It is indeed not at all clear that parody
in any sense was tolerated, but it may perhaps be plausibly held that
in the *Frogs* it is only the public preliminaries to the central rite of
initiation that are parodied. We certainly hear no word of Eleusis
itself or its Telesterion, or of what took place there. Even if this much
be admitted, however, the other objection remains in full force. The
Athenian public would assuredly not have enjoyed an elaborate joke
which emphasised their own very serious plight in a war then at its
most desperate and disastrous stage. In point of fact it is obvious that
other references in the *Frogs* to the war are very gingerly made indeed.

There is a further objection of a major kind to the Eleusinian
interpretation, which has never been satisfactorily met. The procession
of the Blessed which is depicted in the Parodos is but the counterpart
to the series of infernal punishments for the wicked which are
comically described for the intending travellers to Hades by Heracles
earlier in the play (145ff.). Heracles actually tells Dionysos and
Xanthias that the sight of the procession will be their next experience
after they have negotiated the lake of ordure, the stone of withering,
and the fearsome apparition of Empusa. His announcement is itself

of some little importance for the understanding of the Parodos. He
tells the wayfarers that they are to see θιάσους εὐδαίμονας ἀνδρῶν γυναικῶν
(joyous bands of men and women) and these men and women are
in the next line called μεμνημένοι (those who have been initiated).
It has apparently not been noticed that the term θίασοι (a company of
persons dancing and singing in honor of a god) which is paralleled by
θιασώτας in the Parodos itself (327), describes a Dionysiac cult-
association, for which in fact it is one of the technical terms, and that
we have no reason to think Eleusinian initiates ever banded themselves in θίασοι at all. Eleusis was πάγκοινος (common to all) and
was the unique center of its own rites, whereas comparatively small
groups of devotees were typical of the Dionysos-cult, and its ritual
could be celebrated anywhere.

Now there can be no doubt that the infernal punishments, especially the βόρβορος πολύς and the σκῶρ ἀείνων (reeking mire and rip-
pling dung) so lovingly enumerated by Heracles at lines 145-46, are not
derived from Eleusinian doctrine, but from Orphic-Dionysiac sources.
If therefore, in spite of the use of the term θίασοι we interpret the
Heaven of the Parodos as Eleusinian in origin, we must either conclude, as Dieterich does, that the poet made up his account of the
Other-world out of two totally different doctrines, or decide with Maas
that Orphic-Dionysiac and Eleusinian ideas on the subject were identi-
cal in fifth-century Athens. This opinion, however, flies in the face of
all we know about Eleusis, and is rejected by such modern authorities
as Lobeck, Rohde, and Kern. The only other course left open to us
is to recognise that the Iacchos of the *Frogs* cannot be the Eleusinian
divinity, but must be the chthonic Dionysos whom the Orphics worshipped, and that both the Heaven and the Hell described in the play
belong to the teaching involved in his cult.

The Parabasis of the *Frogs*

by *Maurice Croiset*

Between 413 and 404 Athens appears to have displayed a desperate energy. One might think that she would have been downcast after her reverses in Sicily. She had neither fleet nor army left. And yet she held the foe at bay for nine years after that. Neither defeat nor defection could force her to surrender. On two occasions, in 408 and in 406, she seemed to be almost on the point of regaining the upper hand, and she maintained this indomitable resistance to the point of utter exhaustion and at the cost of the most painful sacrifices. At no time, perhaps, in her entire history, did she display a stronger will or a more obstinate courage.

Shall it be said, then, that Aristophanes was mistaken, that under the influence of a prejudice he pointed out imaginary failings? This is hardly credible of a mind which had repeatedly shown itself to be singularly perspicacious. We must be on our guard against permitting ourselves to be misled by appearances.

Nothing is more striking in the behavior of the Athenians at this time than the brusque and, so to speak, sudden character of their decisions. As soon as they are in imminent danger a sort of desperate exaltation possesses them, and they make an extraordinary effort which saves them for the time; but this effort is never sustained. In the main, it almost seems as if they had never had a clear conception of the conditions of success. Was success possible? There is room for doubt. At all events, there was no chance of securing it save on one condition: its enormous difficulties must first be appreciated, and if an earnest attempt was to be made to overcome them, this policy must be backed up by continuity of effort and of sacrifice, which could be secured only by the absolute and unswerving devotion of every citizen to the common cause. It was just such devotion that was lacking. In days of exceptional peril, those who were most energetic or most violent in the assembly carried the others with them, partly through enthusiasm, partly by intimidation. In this way desperate resolutions were taken which had to be carried out subsequently, notwithstanding regrets and attempts at evasion. These were, in a manner, the convulsions of patriotism. Moreover, many private interests were thus satisfied, for the prevailing destitution led many poor people, who were driven to desperation by misery, to take advantage of the opportunity to earn a penny at the expense of allies on whom contributions were levied and of the enemy who were pillaged. Notwithstanding all this, it must be admitted, that true civic spirit was degenerating.

The testimony of Thucydides, Xenophon, and Plato would have to be absolutely rejected, were we disposed to deny the extent to which individualism had been developed in Greece, and especially at Athens, since the beginning of the Peloponnesian War. It had at first spread through the better classes, under the influence of the sophists. Many independent minds, in their search for the foundations of law and ethics, had thought that they rested upon selfish interest. When they sought to make their principles harmonize with their discovery, they even constituted selfish interest, which was often understood in a rather gross sense, their rule of life. Ideas, such as these, when they have once been proclaimed, quickly spread from class to class. Without this quiet revolution, which took place in the days of Aristophanes, there would be no historical explanation for the rather lax morality of the century that followed. Demosthenes hints at it, the new comedy pictures it, and it became crystallized in Epicureanism. Aristophanes witnessed its growth, and he, at least, vaguely understood its seriousness and the causes that led to it. In his eyes, Aeschylus and Euripides, as they are represented in the *Frogs,* stand for the two states of mind through which Athens had passed successively. In this concise and necessarily exaggerated comparison, Euripides stands for restless intellectualism, bent on analysis, incapable, at bottom, of finding satisfaction, but undermining moral discipline because of its inability to assign an indisputable reason for its existence, and consequently giving free scope to the egotistical instincts which fret at social exigencies.

But, after all, did the poet in the *Frogs* wage war on democracy? It seems impossible to maintain that he did. The tendency which he criticizes was really of aristocratic origin. Little by little it had become universal. Aristophanes criticized it freely, without discriminating between classes; but in fact the Athenian aristocracy might have come in for its share of his criticism quite as much as the common people. On the other hand, when considered in the light of its consequences, this tendency was quite as much out of keeping with the democracy as with the aristocracy, if the rule of the majority is indeed the form of government which can least of all get on without the devotion of all to the common cause. The underlying spirit of the *Frogs,* then, is essentially rather ethical and social than, properly speaking, political.

It is true that, side by side with this general thesis, the same play contains some more precise and directly practical counsels of a slightly different character, which finally demand examination.

First, then, there is the famous parabasis, which, according to the anonymous author of the argument, was so much admired by Aristophanes' contemporaries. He informs us, on the testimony of Dicaearchus, that it secured the play the exceptional honor of a second performance. The band of the initiated address the audience through their spokesman, the coryphaeus, and their very character imparts something serious and religious to their counsels; the poet chooses to make a point of this fact. Evidently he does not wish to have his thoughts appear to be the program of a party. He offers them as a sort of solemn instruction, inspired by unselfish patriotism, to men who piously preserve their country's holiest traditions—an instruction which is even, as it were, associated with the celebration of the mysteries.

They say, "It is right that the sacred chorus (τὸν ἱερὸν χορόν) should give the city good counsels and wise instruction. In the first place, we believe in re-establishing equality between citizens, and in putting an end to terror (ἐξισῶσαι τοὺς πολίτας κἀφελεῖν τὰ δείματα). And if any have done wrong, misled by the intrigues of Phrynichus, I declare that they should be allowed to discharge the accusations against them and atone for their former mistakes (αἰτίαν ἐκθεῖσι λῦσαι τὰς πρότερον ἀμαρτίας)" (686-90). The purport of this first injunction is clear. Aristophanes here puts in a claim in the name of a large class of citizens who were at that time treated as suspects, all those, namely, who were suspected of having favored the oligarchy of 411. No charges were lodged against them on this score, which was not of a kind to warrant a legal process; but they were excluded from public functions, or even summoned to court on some pretext, and the democratic tribunals loaded them down with fines. And so, incessantly threatened with ruin, imprisonment, and dishonor, without ever being able to clear themselves of the fundamental, but unavowed, grievance which weighed them down, they endured a veritable reign of terror. It is this odious and lamentable state of affairs, which was well adapted to perpetuate enmity and to keep alive dissensions in the city, that the poet courageously censures in this passage, with a moderation and a candor which do him

great honor. There can be no doubt that he had friends in this perse-
cuted class; but that, after all, is of no great consequence for the ap-
preciation of his words, for he merely asks for justice and equality.
What he claims for them, is the right to clear themselves, the right once
more to become citizens like other people. Unless, indeed, we assume
that hatred and distrust must be the moral temper of a democracy, it is
hard to deny that his advice was compatible with the public weal.

The coryphaeus goes on: "In the second place, I say that no man
who is a citizen of the state should have his civic rights curtailed
(εἶτ' ἄτιμον φημὶ χρῆναι μηδέν' εἶν' ἐν τῇ πόλει). For is not the situation
disgraceful? Certain people here, who were formerly slaves, are ranked
among the Plataeans, because they took part in a single naval battle.
I approve of this reward, to be sure, and have not a word to say
against it; indeed, it is the only sensible thing you have done. But
ought you not, after that, pardon a single unfortunate act of those
who have so many times fought with you at sea, as their fathers have
done before them, and who are of your own race, when they beg for
forgiveness?" (693-99). This passage refers to the citizens who had then
served as hoplites in 411, under the Four Hundred, and who had then
remained at Athens. We know from a statement of Andocides that
they had been placed under a partial ἀτιμία (loss of civil rights), and
had been deprived of the right of speaking in the assembly and of
being elected into the senate. What Aristophanes asks for, therefore,
is the abolition of this punishment, for which, in fact, there was no
possible justification after an interval of six years, and which could
only serve to keep the memory of former dissensions painfully alive.
Sincere and cordial reconciliation in the presence of imminent danger
—that is the essential feature of his program, which he expresses at
the close of this exhortation: "Do ye then, whom nature has made so
clever, allay your anger. Let us seek heartily to win over all our
brothers by recognizing them as citizens, without restriction, as long
as they fight with us on Athenian ships. For if we go on humiliating
them, if we encourage our city in its arrogance and senseless pride,
now when we are at the mercy of the raging waves, I greatly fear that
posterity will condemn us" (700-705).

The second part of the same parabasis goes still further; it may be
regarded as constituting a regular claim in favor of a political party.
I translate it in full: "Many a time we have said to ourselves that
the city treated her best educated citizens (τοὺς καλοὺς τε κἀγαθούς)
as she treats her old coins in relation to her newly minted gold pieces.
We no longer use our old coins, whose alloy was surely not bad, but
which were quite the best of all—the only ones that were honestly

struck and were recognized as excellent everywhere, among Greeks and barbarians, and we prefer this poor copper, coined quite recently and so badly struck. Just so we treat with disdain those of our fellow-citizens whom we know to be of good stock and conduct, just and cultured men, who were educated in the palaestra, in the choruses and in the service of the Muses. But we make every possible use of men of bad alloy, of strangers, of a race of slaves, worthless sons of worthless fathers, Athenians of yesterday, whom the city formerly would never have stooped to use as expiatory victims. Believe me, ye foolish people! Mend your ways and make use once more of respectable men. If you succeed, they will bring you honor. If you fail, good judges will at least say to you that, if you had to be shipwrecked, you did not cling to bad timber while you were drowning" (718-37).

For an entirely clear understanding of the purport of these words, we should have to be much better acquainted than we are with the details of the domestic history of Athens at this time. But, in default of precise facts, there are at least probabilities that we must consider.

Aristophanes in this passage reproaches the people for systematically excluding an entire class of citizens from participation in public affairs, and that on account of their good qualities. Rightly or wrongly, he alleges that the democracy of 405 had a preconceived distrust of well-educated men, and a sort of instinctive leaning toward politicians of the opposite kind. As for the advice he gives, he does not challenge institutions, but merely the manner in which they are administered. He would have the people lend a more willing ear, in the assemblies, to men who were attached to their native soil by solid family interests, by old domestic traditions, and inborn affection, and would have them choose such men to be their generals or their negotiators. Had his purpose been revolutionary, had he conceived the secret plan of substituting an oligarchy for the democracy, it is hard to believe that he would thus have brought it forward in a versified speech, openly delivered in the theater. His counsels could have a practical effect only on two conditions: in the first place, they would have to respond to a latent sentiment that was entertained by a large part of his audience; and, in the second place, they would have to be such as could be adopted without too great difficulty. We may, therefore, conclude that, on the one hand, the facts which he criticizes were at least tacitly admitted to be true by a large part of his audience, and, on the other hand, that his suggestion contained nothing which appeared offensive to them or shocked them. For all these reasons I think the passage just cited ought to be interpreted with the same simplicity with which it was written. We ought not to see anything

more in it than the poet has put into it. Freely and in merry mood
he gives the people good counsel; he does his duty as a conservative
and friend of harmony, and warns the democracy against an exclusive
and intolerant temper. By speaking thus, he virtually urges them to
avoid the catastrophe by which they were to be overwhelmed.

The Character of Dionysus and
the Unity of the *Frogs*

by *Charles Paul Segal*

It has often been remarked that the works of a long-established art-form are the most complex towards the end of its evolution when the form itself is on the verge of disappearing or undergoing a radical transformation. The *Frogs* of Aristophanes provides an excellent illustration of this observation. The last extant example of the true old-comic style and the last of the comedies of Aristophanes performed in the fifth century before the collapse of Athens, the *Frogs* contains a plot of singular complexity, for the poet has combined two types of comic motifs, the journey and the *agon* (contest), each occupying one half of the play. He has also radically altered the traditional structure of Old Comedy by transforming the *agon* that usually takes place before the *parabasis* into a minor scene of little intellectual content (the whipping of Dionysus and Xanthias), whereas the true *agon* occupies the entire second half of the play. This innovation is of some significance for the mood of the play, for in the earlier comedies, notably the *Acharnians* and the *Birds,* the protagonist, victorious in the *agon,* carries out his reforms and remodels the world according to his wishes in the part of the play following the *parabasis.* The *Frogs* lacks this transformation almost entirely; and the *parabasis* is succeeded only by a longer, albeit highly amusing, *agon.*

This lack of a transformation gives the *Frogs* a note of seriousness which befits its subject; but it also raises a problem of a sort, that of the unity of the play and the coherence of such apparently disparate elements as Heracles, the Frog chorus, the Eleusinian Mysteries, Aeschylus and Euripides. Whereas in the earlier plays the magical transformations which succeed the *parabasis* are the logical (or il-

"The Character of Dionysus and the Unity of the Frogs*"* by *Charles Paul Segal.* From Harvard Studies in Classical Philology, *LXV (1961), 207-17; 227-30. Copyright* © *1961 by the President and Fellows of Harvard College. Reprinted by permission of Harvard University Press. Revised by the author for inclusion in this volume.*

logical) extensions of the wish of the protagonist and thus provide a strong unifying theme, the two parts of the *Frogs* are somewhat loosely joined. Dionysus' initial *pothos* or "longing" for Euripides is not ultimately satisfied, and is only indirectly connected with the *agon* between the two tragedians. He is chosen to preside only because he happens to be present at this moment of discord, *stasis*, in Hades (760); and Pluto, aware of the "shortage of clever men" in his realm (806), names Dionysus judge because is is "experienced in the art" (811). The presence of Dionysus alone, therefore, unites the two parts of the play. The forms in which Dionysus himself appears, however, are manifold, and seem at first to enhance even further the impression of incoherence. And yet his disguise as Heracles, his appearance as Iacchus in the Mystic procession, and his role as the god of comedy and tragedy are all ultimately connected and provide a clue to the unity of the play and one of its meanings.

The central problem in the character of Dionysus is how the timorous, almost despicable figure of the first part of the play can serve as arbiter in a contest of the gravest consequences at its end. His development can be followed in some detail and, in fact, permits a glimpse of Aristophanes' remolding of a traditional old-comic motif.

The earliest legends connected with Dionysus have already an element of the potentially ridiculous or incongruous about them that made them suitable for comic treatment. The description of the frightened god fleeing to Thetis in the *Iliad* is perhaps not without a touch of humor (6.135-37):

> Dionysus, terrified, went down through the waves of the sea; and Thetis received him in her bosom. For strong was the trembling that seized him at the shouting of the hero Lycurgus.

The incongruity between the effeminacy of the god and his dangerous power has a potentially comic side which appears also in the Homeric Hymn to Dionysus (VII) and, though more grimly, even in Euripides' *Bacchae*. The satyr-plays, of course, such as the *Lycurgus* of Aeschylus, would have presented Dionysus in a still more comic light; and the god so appears in Euripides' *Cyclops*. In the course of the discussion of Odysseus and the Cyclops on the nature of Dionysus, the Cyclops asks, "How can a god take pleasure in dwelling in wine-skins?" and remarks, "A god should not keep his body in wine-skins" (527). Such is the profligate and bibulous nature of this god. Comedy has thus only to combine some of these motifs and shift their emphasis in order to produce the desired ludicrous effect.

Old Comedy seems, in fact, to have exploited just this ridiculous aspect of the god. He appears as a gluttonous, licentious braggart whose real cowardliness is quickly shown up at the first test, a typical ancient *miles gloriosus*. Eupolis in his *Taxiarchoi* doubtless exploited this aspect of Dionysus in depicting him learning the art of war from Phormio in Hades, but unwilling to renounce certain pleasures. The comic poet, Platon, in the *Adonis* played upon the sensuality of Dionysus by making him a rival with Aphrodite for her famous favorite, whose approaching birth is announced in oracles, a possible parody of the rivalry of Poseidon and Zeus for Thetis. The most important evidence for the treatment of Dionysus in Old Comedy, however, derives from the ancient summary of the *Dionysalexandros* of Cratinus discovered in a papyrus fragment at the beginning of this century. Here Dionysus revealed his amorous propensities in replacing Paris as judge of the three goddesses. Naturally he chooses Aphrodite in order to win Helen as his reward. His braggadocio and timorousness were probably displayed at the arrival of the Greeks, when the frightened god tries to hide Helen and disguise himself as a ram. It is possible, however, that he defied the Greeks heroically before their arrival, his desire momentarily conquering his fear; and the scene might have resembled the reaction of the Aristophanic Dionysus at the promise of the dancing girls (516) who await the "true" Heracles. There would have been supplications and prayers to the rescuers and to Paris, making the god appear even more ridiculous; and this scene was perhaps similar to Dionysus' entreaties to his "Xanthidion" in the *Frogs* to re-exchange costumes when the inn-keeping woman and Plathane threaten (579ff.).

From the beginning of the *Frogs*, however, another quality makes itself evident which shows that Aristophanes is not merely reproducing the stock comic Dionysus. His is a god with "longing" for Euripides, an intellectual seeking a "clever poet" (71), who cannot be dissuaded from his other-worldly quest. In the opening lines he strictly forbids Xanthias to use the worn-out comic jokes of the stage-slave. He is not content with mere buffoonery any more than he is with the empty chattering of Euripides' successors (89ff.).

It is primarily in his relation to Heracles that his differentiation from the comic Dionysus of Cratinus appears. He has, on the one hand, a certain affinity with Heracles. They are, of course, brothers and address one another in intimate terms (60). Dionysus plans to imitate Heracles and does so not only in the descent itself, but also in the matter of servitude (cf. Heracles' enslavement to Omphale). They are, furthermore, traditionally associated with one another as the two gods most ridiculed and degraded by the writers of Old Comedy. Julian speaks of "the comic poets insulting and dragging around Heracles and Dionysus" (*Misopogon,* 366c). Yet it would be

expected that these two gods of strong sensual appetites would understand one another better than they in fact do. Dionysus adopts a
rather scornful attitude to Heracles' gluttony when Heracles reveals
his complete insensitivity to the superior art of Euripides (89ff.). He
finds his *pothos* or "longing" entirely misunderstood by Heracles,
who immediately refers it to a woman or boy or, finally, to Cleisthenes
(56ff.). He has difficulty in expressing the ethereal nature of his longing
to his coarser brother, and finally has to resort to the analogy of soup
(60ff.). Aristophanes has detached the intellectual element in Dionysus
and set it in contrast to Heracles, to whom he also transfers most of
the gluttony usually associated with Dionysus. Hence the incongruity
of Dionysus' disguise as Heracles is all the greater because Dionysus
not only lacks Heracles' military prowess, but is divested also of his
model's devotion to mere physical appetite. This differentiation of
Heracles and Dionysus, of course, is only partial; and the comedy
would lose much of its vitality if it proceeded any further. But a
higher note in Dionysus' character, an almost Euripidean "otherness"
—to use Dodds' term—is sounded from the very beginning and prepares for the conception of Dionysus in the second half of the play.

The object of Dionysus' journey to Hades appears, in fact, as the
testing of the Heraclean side of his nature. It soon becomes apparent
that the results of this test are negative; and the unfortunate results
of Dionysus' disguise as Heracles are analogous to his prohibition of
Xanthias' indulgence in the common slave-tricks of contemporary
comic poets: both imply the inadequacy of a conception of the comic
limited to mere buffoonery.

Dionysus appears as the embodiment of the comic spirit seeking a
stable definition of itself and its aims. His search is presented primarily
through the motifs of disguise and changeability. With the assump-
tion of a new garment comes the testing of a new identity and the
beginning of a transformation of character. Here again Aristophanes
is working within the bounds of a traditional theme. To disguise the
protagonist as his apparent opposite is a regular *modus operandi* of
Old Comedy, familiar from the remodeling of Mnesilochus as a woman
in the *Thesmophoriazousae*; and there is an even more immediate tradition in the *Dionysalexandros* of Cratinus, where the god seems to
have been disguised as Paris and even as a ram. But the Aristophanic
Dionysus feels singularly out of place in his new garb. Not only does
he provoke the laughter of Heracles himself (42ff.), but he fails to
adapt to his new surroundings. Here he stands in marked contrast to
his slave, Xanthias, the forerunner of the facile slave or parasite of
New Comedy. Thus Dionysus is uncertain about how the natives of
Hades knock on doors (46off.), while Xanthias simply tells him, "Keep

a figure (*schēma*) and a mind (*lēma*) like Heracles' " (463). It is, however, precisely this lack of correspondence between *schēma* and *lēma* which is the cause of Dionysus' failure.

This lack of correspondence between appearance and reality, external posture and inner disposition, is the source of the instability of Dionysus. He exchanges roles with Xanthias four times in two hundred lines; and after the first set of exchanges the chorus sings an ode on the cleverness of changeability, "to turn about to the softer way" (*pros to malthakōteron*) in preference to assuming one *schēma* (533ff.). When Xanthias reassumes the Heraclean costume, however, the chorus too reverses itself completely and warns him not to commit anything *malthakon,* "soft" (533ff.). Xanthias similarly ridicules the changeability of his master by remarking ironically to the Hostess and Plathane on the gluttonous and ruffian ways of the pseudo-Heracles, "It's his work all right; that's his manner *everywhere*" (563).

Dionysus' continual shifting of disguises reflects the weakness of the comic spirit itself at the time, the failure of the external boisterousness of comedy such as practiced by Phrynichus, Lykis, and Ameipsias (13ff.) when its bases in a firm and stable communal life and a clear conception of its own end are lacking. Dionysus as the comic spirit has the vestiges of a Heraclean vitality, and the reputation of his predecessor follows him—to his discomfort—all along his journey. And yet the lion-skin of Heracles is betrayed by the *kothornoi* (557), and it is perhaps more than just the exigencies of the comic situation that cause him to be accepted as Heracles only when he is to suffer for his model's misdeeds. The low comic buffoonery with which Xanthias is associated from the very beginning adapts easily enough to the role of Heracles. But for Dionysus a more stabilizing, unifying principle is sought, one that will enable him to maintain some of the comic vitality which Heracles possesses without stooping to the low tricks which he apparently detests and to which he is, in fact, proved unsuited. Comedy as entertainment has apparently become separated from comedy as a potentially didactic medium, which it was in Aristophanes' earlier plays.

The reunification of these two aspects of comedy is, in part, the quest of Dionysus and takes the form of a reintegration of his own personality. His problem, on the literary level, is to be able both to amuse and instruct, to appear in the age of the degenerate Phrynichus, Lykis, and Ameipsias as he did in the days of the "bull-eating" Cratinus. Hence there is a real kinship between Dionysus' development in the first part of the play and the issues of the *agon* in the second part: the faults of Euripides as analyzed by Aeschylus and the assertion of the communal function and dignity of the tragic poet are thematically related to the weakness of the purely "Heracleioxanthian" conception of comedy and to Dionysus' *pothos* and search in Hades for something that has passed out of the world of the living and is to be found only in the land of the dead.

The breakdown of the communal solidarity which the battle of Arginusae and its aftermath exposed requires drastic measures, and the god of comedy must strip himself of his previous identity in order to arrive at a positive conception of himself which will meet the new demands put upon him. Hence, when he first descends as Heracles, he fails to recognize "himself" when the frogs sing of "Nyseian Dionysus the son of Zeus in Limnae" (215ff.), or when the Mystae sing of Iacchus. This failure to acknowledge himself as Nyseian Dionysus or Iacchus does not necessarily mean, as some commentators have felt, that the different aspects of the god were kept separate and simply not thought of together (in fact, the opposite is true), but merely that Dionysus-Heracles has not yet attained the unified conception of himself which he is seeking and thus *cannot* yet acknowledge his identity as Iacchus. He must, in fact, relinquish his traditional divinity in order to regain a sounder dignity.

Hence he not only forbids Xanthias to call him "Dionysus," but he extends the injunction to the name "Heracles" as well (298ff.). Thus he temporarily loses all identity. Not only does he exchange roles with his slave, but he endures the basest of necessities of slavery, physical punishment, and an accuser's right of torture (616, 625, 629). The pain which he unsuccessfully tries to conceal, furthermore, is an indication of his loss of divinity: "For if he's god," says Xanthias (634), "he won't feel it." In another sense too Dionysus' reduction to the role of slave is the fullest possible execution of the *mimesis* of Heracles, whose slavery to Omphale was regarded as the most debasing of his toils. Yet under the duress of this final episode, Dionysus does begin to reaccept his divinity and the dignity it entails. He challenges the claim of Xanthias to torture him, proclaiming, "I forbid any one to torture me, as I am immortal" (628-29), and, "I claim that I am immortal, Dionysus, the son of Zeus" (631). Contrast his identification of himself at the beginning of the play as "Dionysus, son of Winejar" (22). It is perhaps significant that here in 631 he uses the formula used by the frogs when they sang of Dionysus in Limnae ("Dionysus, son of Zeus," 216). He thus associates himself with the established communal and cult implications of his divinity. In so doing, he points toward a vision of what comedy might be, a reflection of the solidarity of the community, firm in its ancient cults. He is then ready for the Aeschylean conception of tragedy in the second part of the play.

Dionysus' reattainment of his divinity may even bear some resemblance to the actual Mystae, who, after seeing a vision of the under-world and the punishment of the wicked, arise to a new, semi-divine condition as initiates. Dionysus' progress in Hades is in part negative, for he casts off finally the disguise which he initially adopted. By the end of the first *agon*, the trial before Aeacus, Dionysus has thus returned to his starting point. But he has in the process succeeded in stripping off a partially false and inadequate conception of himself when, at the command of Aeacus (641), he and Xanthias strip off their false garments and stand, presumably naked, before one of the judges of the underworld.

After the *parabasis*, with its exhortation to the sacred chorus to advise and teach what is *chrēsta*, "good for the city" (686f.), Dionysus has, in fact, attained a new dignity. His recognition by Pluto and Persephone soon entails his serving as judge on what is essentially the problem of the relation of art and literature to the state; and this very appointment is indicative of his now recognized position as the god of the communal dramatic festivals. He executes his task admirably, though of course with some buffoonery. He is not merely the stock figure of the *agon*, a ridiculous third party, as Cornford sees him, present only to exploit the comic possibilities of the scene, but does perform a very valuable function. Despite his initial *pothos* for Euripides, he manages to remain a fair and impartial judge. Thus he tries to induce Aeschylus to speak in his own defence against Euripides' attack (832), he restrains Euripides' loquacity (835) and Aeschylus' wrath (844ff.), and is delighted in turn by each of the accusations and rebuttals (1150ff.), even though he admits that he cannot follow all of Euripides' reasoning (1169). Though a supposed Euripides-lover, he defends Aeschylus spontaneously, before the poet can even defend himself (1175ff.). When the two tragedians begin to quarrel, he interjects his own newly gained conception of the dignity of poetry: "It is unfitting for men who are poets to exchange insults like bakers' wives" (857-58). He thus criticizes implicitly such scenes as he himself experienced in the first part of the play with the Hostess and Plathane (or such as occur at the end of the *Wasps*). And at the end, after his decision, he even succeeds in remaining clever and dignified in the face of Euripides' insults.

In the light of the development of Dionysus, his ultimate choice of Aeschylus is not so surprising after all. Dionysus, in fact, confesses that he enjoyed the old Aeschylean dramas "no less than the present prattlers" (916f.), and that he cannot follow all Euripides' subtle quibblings (1169). He sympathizes with Euripides' troubles with the *lekythion*, "the little bottle of oil" (1220ff.), but clearly indicates that Aeschylus has fairly won the Battle of the Prologues (1245ff.). Yet Dionysus, doubtless like Aristophanes himself, obviously admires the skill (*dexiotēs*) and cleverness (*sophia*) of Euripides: "For I think the one clever (*sophon*); but I enjoy the other" (1412). Dionysus' rejection of Heracles and the low comic tricks of Xanthias is in fact an attempt to take *sophia* and *dexiotēs* into account. These two words are not always pejorative, for Aristophanes uses them of his own achievement in the *Clouds* and *Wasps*. Cratinus even coined the word "Euripidaristophanize" (fr. 307). Hence in rejecting the pure buffoonery of Heracles and the earlier conception of himself, Dionysus at least leaves room for *sophia* in his attitude toward the poet, although he is not willing to sacrifice to it the sense of the communal mission of the poet which Aeschylus represents.

The recognition of Dionysus as the god of the stable and secure community results almost immediately in the re-establishment of order in Hades. The situation of Hades is, of course, analogous to that "among the corpses of the upper world." Hades is disturbed by great "civic discord" (*stasis*, 760), just like the world above (359), caused primarily by the agitation of the coarser element for Euripides: "The good element (*chrēston*) is in the minority, just as it is there above" (783). The arrival of Dionysus puts an end to this confusion and bolsters the better element in the state (*to chrēston*) by the choice of Aeschylus, who represents the more conservative, traditional outlook of the unified community and in fact did not get along well with the more developed Athenian democracy (807ff.).

Dionysus' re-establishment of communal order is largely expressed through the theme of slave-master relations, a natural image to use after Arginusae (cf. 190, 694). In the *parabasis* the chorus complains that it is disgraceful for those who fought in but one sea-battle to be honored like the staunch Plataeans and become "lords instead of slaves" (693-94). This reversal of the traditional situation is, of course, analogous to the charge that Athens raises its lower element to positions of leadership and power, while "the better element" (*hoi chrēstoi*) are merely set aside (718ff., 1443ff.). The reversal of the position of the slaves, however, bears a closer relation to Dionysus' own experiences, for he and Xanthias do exchange roles as master and slave; and the little *agon* which precedes the *parabasis* centers about the discovery of the actual slave.

In the early part of the *agon*, the slave has the upper hand. His ostensible generosity in letting Aeacus torture the pseudo-Xanthias is called a "noble deed" (*gennaion pragma*) (615), and he himself "a noble man" (*gennadas anēr*) (640), words which recur elsewhere throughout the play to identify the superior element in the state. When the final identification is made, however, Aeacus recognizes that Dionysus is the master (*despotēs*) and the *gennadas anēr* (738). The recognition between Pluto and Dionysus has its counterpart in that of Xanthias and Aeacus, who swear friendship "by Zeus, our Lord of the whip" (756); and their joining of right hands (754) points ahead to the similar token of kinship between Sophocles and Aeschylus (789). Through Dionysus' rediscovery of his identity, in other words, the proper separation is made between "the better element" (*to chrēston*) and the low-born (*to doulikon*), and each element is to go its own way. The slave element disappears after Dionysus' attainment of his true divinity and his appointment as judge, though it predominated in the first part of the play.

The final defeat of Euripides marks the full restoration of order, for Euripides is charged with having confused and upset domestic relations in the same way as occurred at Arginusae and in Dionysus' cortège. Aristophanes alludes to his exploitation of his slave Cephisophon in writing his tragedies "mixing in a bit of Cephisophon" (944) and, indeed, to the gossip about Cephisophon's seduction of Euripides' wife (1048, 1408). Euripides too has made the slave as loquacious as his master (948ff.) and has introduced an atmosphere of suspicion into the Athenian household (980ff.). The discrepancy between language and sentiment in Euripides which Aeschylus opposes (1053ff.), a divorcement between style and content perhaps reflected in the application of the *lekythion,* "the little bottle of oil," is also related to the disorder and lack of harmony between the parts of the state; and here too the Euripidean outlook, as Aristophanes sees it, is responsible.

The structure of the *Frogs* is thus somewhat analogous after all to that of the earlier plays where the victory of the Agonist resulted in a transformation of his environment. Dionysus' victory in the small *agon* before the *parabasis* does result in a kind of transformation of Hades, an image of the order which Aristophanes would like to see transferred to the upper world. As in the earlier plays too, where the protagonist enjoys the fruits of his victory after the *agon,* so in the *Frogs* the increased dignity of Dionysus, his appointment as judge, and the full recognition of his divinity are all the happy results of his victory. But Hades is still Hades, and no large-scale imaginative transformation of the external world occurs.

The play ends in rebirth; and the rebirth of Aeschylus is linked with that of Dionysus, for they are both to ascend to the upper world together, like the saved Mystae. And yet Dionysus' rebirth, his rediscovery of himself, contains from the start a negative element in his recognition by the chthonic powers, Pluto and Persephone. The corpse whom he meets at the beginning of the journey (170ff.)—a peculiarly

Athenian corpse at that, demanding an exorbitant two drachmas for
a petty task—is symbolic of the spiritual death of the Athenians, who
are only corpses in the upper world (424). It thus hints at the ultimate
failure of the broader implications of Dionysus' mission. Dionysus was
reborn only through a radical self-modification, a kind of self-destruc-
tion, of which the Athenians are no longer capable, for the transformation involved lies beyond their spiritual powers.

Whatever possibility for an actual regeneration there is, however, is
to come through the communal aspect of Dionysus. It is, therefore, perhaps instructive to consider briefly in this context Aristophanes' relation to the treatment of Dionysus in the *Bacchae* of Euripides, written
within a year or two of the *Frogs*. There is good reason to believe that
Aristophanes knew Euripides' play and may even be alluding to it in
several passages. In so far as the *Bacchae* may be regarded as a defense
of the divinity of Dionysus and an attempt to return to simpler and
more immediate forms of belief, there may be perhaps, paradoxically,
some basic similarity with the *Frogs*. Both works would then appear to
arise from a concern with a declining belief in the power of the gods
and the power of the myth. And yet the difference lies precisely in
the types of Dionysus presented in the two plays. The god of the
Bacchae is the orgiastic Dionysus, essentially asocial, a dangerous god,
quick to punish offenses upon his divinity. Defiance of his worship
produces individual convulsions that shake the state and negate accepted social values. In this sense, the *Bacchae* represents the most extreme development of the forces of individualism. Those forces, always inherent in the nature of Greek tragedy, now become the directing
motives of the plot.

Against this universal, individualistic, orgiastic god, who manifests
himself in subjective illusion, Aristophanes sets the Athenian god of
comedy, closely attached to the communal festivals where all the re-
pressed eroticism of a Pentheus has free vent in such moments as that
of the Eleusinian procession (411ff.). There is almost a deliberate attempt to free Dionysus from the dangerous elements that appear in
the *Bacchae*. As a stock figure in Old Comedy, he will endure insults
of all kinds, even being whipped as a slave, very much unlike Euripides'
Dionysus, who explains as the cause of all the destruction he has
wrought: "I, a god, received insult (*hybris*) at your hands" (*Bacch.*
1348; cf. *Frogs* 21). Hence Aristophanes is careful to exclude the orgiastic god from a significant part in the comedy, and, naturally, plays
upon the innocent braggadocio and love of women and wine that char-
acterize the god in Old Comedy. Dionysus even gives his initial judgments on the contemporary tragedians in language befitting the wine-
god (92ff.). Aristophanes harps upon his timidity and lets his associa-

tion with the more serious side of his cult as a vegetation-god appear only indirectly.

The difference between the Dionysus of each play, then, is a significant indication of the gap between the comic and the tragic outlook, between social man's joyful acceptance of his limitations and individual man's agonizing struggle with them. In tragedy death is the supreme trial of life and exhausts the hero's energies, showing him empty or confirming his strength. In the comic *Frogs* death yields. The most inflexible of mortal realities gives way. Dionysus' "longing" brings back from the realm of death the needed poet-teacher; and he finds in Aeschylus, dead for fifty years, a poet more truly *gonimos*— "creative," "life-giving" (96)—than the recently alive Euripides whom he originally sought. The Dionysus of the *Frogs* is a god of life through whom rebirth triumphs in the face of death, community in the face of dissolution and selfishness, Aeschylean staunchness in the face of Euripidean divisive cleverness.

It is this inclusive vitality of Dionysus which leaps the gap between life and death, comedy and tragedy, and enables him to reconcile such disparate elements as the frog-chorus and the Mystae, Iacchus and the wine-god. The play revolves about dichotomies which are reflected in its bipartite structure; and it is only the full development of the character of Dionysus which enables him to absorb both the low comedy of the first part and the serious issues of the second half of the play. Dionysus thus presents a statement of the solidarity of the community in men's ability to laugh and play together as well as to work and face the "serious" issues of life. Thus it is that in a comedy he can pronounce judgments on the tragic poets, and he most truly appears in the last scene as the god of *both* comedy and tragedy.

His unified personality, then, embraces all the choral elements in the play. Especially important is a song of the Mystae, who pray to Demeter: "Grant me to say much that is funny (*geloia*), but also much that is serious (*spoudaia*)" (391-92). This alternation of *geloion* and *spoudaion*, the laughable and the serious, provides one of the main unifying motifs of the play. The comedy begins with Xanthias' request to say something "at which the spectators always laugh" (*gelōsi*), and Dionysus' refusal already creates the essential dichotomy of the play. But a little later it is Dionysus himself who arouses the inextinguishable "laughter," *gelōs*, of Heracles (42ff.). When Dionysus has regained some of the balance between *gelōs* and *spoudē*, however, after his recognition, the low-comic element, as represented by the slaves Xanthias and Aeacus, departs from the stage in deference to the seriousness, *spoudē*, of their masters: "When our masters get serious, there's trouble for us" (812).

The proper combination of laughter and seriousness is symbolic of the unity of the *polis* and appears in the songs of the Mystae, where the seriousness of the religious ritual is relieved by the licentious good-fellowship of the procession. The prayer for "dance and play" (390), in the same strophic system in which the *geloia-spoudaia* dichotomy is developed, may also reflect this binary aspect of the Mystic procession and, indeed, of the whole comedy: the combination of the sheer enjoyment of licentious banter and playfulness for its own sake with the more serious sense of the ritual-communal act of the dance. It is this *double* attitude toward the gods, as opposed to the inflexible, one-directional view of tragedy, that makes comedy, and the *Frogs* especially, the exponent of a fully livable, even if in practice unattained, integration of the gods into the community. Snell, in the Aristophanes' chapter of his *Discovery of the Mind,* has well characterized this aspect of Greek "piety":

> We find it difficult to understand how the gods of one's faith could be subjected to Aristophanic jests. But the laughter is part of the meaning, the fruitfulness, the positive side of life, and it is, therefore, in the eyes of the Greeks, more godlike than the sour solemnity which we associate with piety.

The search of the spirit of comedy to find its proper relation to the community and the gods is thus completed at the end of the play in the fully developed communal aspect of Dionysus; and what emerges is, in fact, a definition applicable to tragedy as well. The second half of the play shows Aristophanes' renewed consciousness of the equality of the tragic and comic poet in their educative function: both teachers of their *polis* and both serving but different aspects of a single, unified divine nature. The process of Dionysus' development can thus be regarded as the central and unifying theme of the play. He succeeds in integrating the old-comic buffoon with the god of the dramatic festivals. Into this wider conception of himself as the god of the festive aspect of communal life he absorbs also his various other religious functions, including his somewhat more solemn and serious side as Iacchus. The festal procession thus becomes a leitmotif of the play, itself both an enactment and a symbol of communal solidarity. The theme of rebirth also concerns the regeneration of the *polis* through this general attempt to unify religion and art, Iacchus and Dionysus, as complementary, closely fitting expressions of a healthy communal life. The asocial, orgiastic Dionysus of the *Bacchae* is rejected, along with the entire Euripidean outlook, as being hostile to this spirit of communal regeneration.

The *Frogs,* in a way, can be regarded as a defense of Old Comedy itself, which could flourish only in the atmosphere of confidence in the unity of the *polis* which Aristophanes is attempting to promote. Aristophanes seems to sense the imminent collapse of Athens, and tries to make a final defense of an art-form which, more than any other, is inseparable from its communal setting. His concern with the imagery of death and resurrection, however, suggests that he also sensed the futility of his effort.

A View of Euripides

by Gilbert Murray

Aristophanes was after all first and foremost a man of letters. As a writer of comedy he was σοφός (clever) and could not altogether get on with the spectators who were not σοφοί also. His first quarrel with the new education was its neglect of literature. Even his politics are the politics of a literary man, greatly moved by the spirit of a policy, its cruelty, its unfairness, its vulgarity, and not so much by its results. His wildest scenes of farce never get far away from literature; they abound in parodies and quotations and are often actually founded on some scene in a tragedy. He quotes, at a rough calculation, no less than twenty-one writers, mostly poets, of previous generations, from Homer to Aeschylus, and mentions about double that number of contemporaries. He loved all poetry; he loved perverting it and laughing at it. But above all poetry he knew by heart and quoted and parodied and mocked at the tragedies of Euripides.

One must always remember that Comedy originated in a traditional half-magic ritual, one of those rites, common to most primitive societies, which are themselves part of the sacred laws and customs by which our fathers lived, and which make it their aim and their excuse to preserve those laws and customs. To honor and obey the City's Gods, the City's laws, and one's own parents, was, according to Greek traditional ideas, the whole duty of man. To do so was Themis: to fail to do so was a breach of Themis, and might have quite unpredictable consequences. Hence Aristophanes, and, as far as we can judge, the other comedians, are normally defenders of the established custom, and satirize all that is new or unusual. Hence also the chief character in Aristophanes is almost always an Old Man, a γέρων, who knows and likes the old ways, whereas young men, poor creatures, usually do not know what is Themis and what not! It is only natural, therefore, that Comedy finds it obvious prey in new teachers, like Socrates, in inno-

---

"A View of Euripides." From Aristophanes *by Gilbert Murray (Oxford: The Clarendon Press, 1933). Copyright 1933 by the Clarendon Press. Reprinted by permission of the publisher. Original notes omitted from this essay by permission of the Clarendon Press, Oxford.*

vating poets, like Euripides, in startling ideas, like this fancy of philosophers about the equality of women and men.

It is difficult for us, and would have been difficult for Aristophanes himself, to say exactly what his feelings were towards Euripides and his poetry. He certainly was fascinated by it. It haunted his memory and imagination, and he parodied it with a charm and skill which prove his enjoyment and understanding. At the same time he almost certainly disapproved of it, or at least felt officially bound to disapprove of it, just as he disapproved of Socrates, and the sophistic movement in general, and all this nonsense about women . . . though, to be sure, if women had their way, Greece might still be saved! So he writes the *Clouds*, and the *Lysistrata*, and diligently studies Euripides till a rival comedian, Cratinus, mocks at him for writing in the same refined, epigrammatic over-intellectual style, and coins the word 'Euripidaristophaism.'

Considering the extreme generosity with which Aristophanes distributes personal abuse when so disposed, it is interesting to note that there is no attack on the personal character or honor of Euripides. We observed the same with regard to Socrates. One of the less pleasing accusations which are freely tossed about in the Old Comedy, for example, is that of personal immorality. It is probably part of the phallic ritual, and means little. It is flung most emphatically at Agathon, for example, when he is found rehearsing his verses at the opening of the *Thesmophoriazusae*, but the insult did not prevent Aristophanes from being one of the chosen guests at Agathon's famous Symposium, nor from passing the kindly judgment upon him in the *Frogs*: 'A true poet, whom his many friends miss deeply.' So it is the more striking that no personal attack of that sort, or indeed of any other sort, is made against Euripides: no charge of immorality, of softness, of taking bribes, of avarice, of cowardice, of 'sycophancy,' or anything else. The most that one can say is that in the contest with Aeschylus in the *Frogs* Euripides is made rather conceited and unpleasant.

We possess three plays in which Euripides comes in for special attention. In 425 B.C., at the opening of his career as a comedian, Aristophanes devotes one whole scene of the *Acharnians* to him. Fifteen years later, in the *Thesmophoriazusae*, he creates scene after scene of ingenious farce almost entirely out of lines from three Euripidean tragedies. Lastly, in 405, after the poet's death, Aristophanes represents the God of Drama, Dionysus, as descending to Hades to fetch Euripides back, since he is unable to live without him, but eventually deciding that, if one and one only of the great poets of the past is to come back, he would sooner have Aeschylus. This play gives Aristophanes occasion to make a long study of Euripides' work as a dramatic poet, and to enrich us with the liveliest and most intimate piece of literary criticism that has come down from antiquity. . . .

What was, then, at the end of the count, Aristophanes' real opinion about Euripides? He had quoted him, advertised him, laughed at him and with him for so many years, and at last the great poet was dead and his place empty. In 405 Aristophanes tried to sum up what he had to say about Euripides. It is a surprise to us, when we think of it, to realize that an Athenian audience could sit through long scenes of literary criticism and parody devoted to the comparison of two dead tragedians, and at the end not merely pronounce the play worthy of the first prize, but actually insist on a repetition of the performance a few days later. The *Frogs* was probably the greatest success Aristophanes ever achieved, yet he clearly knew the risk he was running. The *Clouds* had been above the heads of the audience; will not this be more so? 'No,' he makes the Chorus say: 'if you fear that the audience may be a little stupid, and miss the points of your subtleties, do not be anxious: that is no longer likely. They have been through the training. Every one of them has his book, and understands what is good taste.' The whole intellectual level of the audience had risen; Aristophanes, the intellectual farce-writer, has profited by it; and the cause of the whole improvement has been that 'new learning' of which Euripides is the champion.

What is the main plot of the *Frogs*? When the *Frogs* was writing, it would appear, Sophocles was still alive, though he died before the actual performance. But Euripides was dead, and the world seemed empty and tasteless without him—at least that was the feeling of Dionysus, the divine patron of drama. He must have a poet—a real poet with power to create (γόνιμον ποιητήν) and will to dare. He goes to Hades to bring back Euripides, and, after many adventures, arrives there to find a contest going on between Euripides and the ancient Aeschylus, who has held the Throne of Poetry ever since his death. The contest proceeds, with Dionysus as judge. There is mutual criticism of the general style of both poets; then of prologues; then of lyrics of various kinds; then of the weight of individual verses. Still, Dionysus will not decide. He loves both men. He wants to be friends with both. One is so accomplished (σοφός), and he does so enjoy the other. At last, in the hope of getting more light, he asks the two their advice about the public affairs of Athens; the question is not entirely irrelevant, since both rivals have accepted the view that a poet is to be judged by his wisdom and the advice he gives (1009). The pressing problem of the moment is Alcibiades. What do the two poets say about him? Euripides condemns the man who 'is slow to help and quick to injure his country, rich in resources for himself and bankrupt for her.'

Aeschylus differs: 'It is wiser not to rear a lion's whelp; but if you have reared one, you must accept its ways.' The judge is still doubtful. What advice have they for the City; how can she be saved? 'Put your trust where mistrust is,' says Euripides, 'and mistrust where you now put trust.' That is, turn out the present advisers and call back the wiser, more cultivated and more moderate leaders—whom Aristophanes also believed in. And what says Aeschylus? 'Treat the enemy's land as yours, and yours as the enemy's; your ships as your treasure and your "new treasure" as despair.' The words are an expression of the old policy of Pericles (*Thuc.*, i. 143) suited for more prosperous times than 405. At any rate they clearly imply war *jusqu'au bout*. Live on your enemy's land, think no more about your own, put all your hopes in your fleet, and—apparently, though not certainly—recognize that you are financially ruined and that the new special taxes will bring no help.

'Come, give your decision,' says Pluto. And Dionysus, with a plunge, giving up the attempt at a critical judgment, says he will choose the one he happens to like: Aeschylus! One can hardly imagine a closer contest; and when one realizes that the contest is for the supreme throne of poetry it is difficult to suppose that the *Frogs* was written as a mere attack on Euripides or an attempt to show that he was a bad poet. William James speaks somewhere of a man who threatened suicide because he was only the second-best baseball 'striker' in the world; only by such a standard as that can the *Frogs* be regarded as a condemnation of Euripides. It is something far more natural and far more interesting. Euripides was dead; the world seemed empty of poetry. Oh, if one could go down to the grave and bring him back! And yet, if one could do that; if one could bring back from Hades one poet and only one, would it be Euripides, or are there greater poets still? Is there not he whom we loved and worshipped in childhood, old-fashioned perhaps and despised by the critics of today, not quite to be defended on sophisticated modern standards, but still incomparable, the King of poets, Aeschylus!

So much for the general scheme of the play; but there are also a great number of minute and definite criticisms which have to be considered. Some are mere jokes; for of course we must remember that we are dealing not merely with a comedy, but a comedy in the ancient sense—a wild though highly intellectual farce—and cannot take all its quips seriously. For example, it is said that the burglars and thieves were all on the side of Euripides because of τῶν ἀντιλογιῶν καὶ λυγισμῶν καὶ στροφῶν (771), where στροφαί means both 'twists' and 'strophes,' λυγισμοί both 'changing tones of voice' and 'wrestling tricks,' and the ἀντιλογίαι or 'controversies' in which Euripides excelled are very different from the 'denials' with which the said criminals liked to meet accusations. Similarly when Aeschylus refuses to compete on the ground that his poetry has not died with him, so that he has none by him, while that of Euripides is all dead and handy, it is a joke and no more (869).

Another quite absurd joke has been taken seriously by commentators. Euripides is quoting his prologues, and Aeschylus threatens to destroy the whole lot of them with a ληκύθιον, or 'oil-flask,' of the sort that was commonly carried and served both for anointing the body and for mixing paints. Euripides quotes seven prologues, and in six of them, before he has finished the third line, Aeschylus interjects the words ληκύθιον ἀπώλεσε, 'lost his little flask of oil,' so as to complete both sense and meter.

The effect is very funny, but the criticism amounts to nothing. Scholars say that it indicates the monotony of Euripides' versification, but this is simply not the case. As a matter of fact, of the seven prologues quoted the seventh—the funniest—does not really work; the sixth, according to the Scholiast, was not taken from the beginning of the *Meleager*, but from a passage some way on; the first did not agree with the version of *Archelaus* which the Scholiast knew. And further, among the tragedies that have come down to us the ληκύθιον tag does not fit the openings of Euripides any more than those of Sophocles or Aeschylus. There is, as criticism, simply nothing in it; yet, such was the influence of this scene that the particular meter of ληκύθιον ἀπώλεσε, i.e., the second part of an iambic trimeter after the ordinary caesura (-◡-◡-◡-, 'found his old umbrella gone') was subsequently called not only ληκύθιον, which was more or less justified, but Εὐριπίδειον, which was absurd.

As for the serious criticisms, they are hard to seize, but in the main they resolve themselves into breaches of Themis and the consequent incongruities. The two spheres in which all primitive societies are specially subject to taboos are religion and sex, and Euripides, like Socrates, was not satisfied with the Greek conventions about either. Then tragedy itself was in origin a religious rite which ought according to Themis to be composed in a certain way, whereas Euripides was always making experiments with it. True, he was very intellectual and full of conscious artistic principles; but . . . well, Aristophanes really preferred Aeschylus, who simply wrote as he ought, without knowing why.

The idea of scientific literary criticism was new and 'Euripidean.' He would weigh the poetry line by line; measure it with straight edges, miter-squares, cubit-rules and frames . . . a method which made Aeschylus 'stoop and glower like a mad bull.' He would produce work

that was ἀστεῖον, *urbanum*, κατερρινημένον, *lima perpolitum;* above all,
lucid (900ff., 945ff., 1122); whereas Aeschylus wrote for an audience
fresh from Phrynichus and only half-civilized. His diction, though far
more varied than that of Aeschylus, tries to be appropriate: he would
not use the word ἀλεκτρυών, cock, in a tragedy, as Aeschylus did. And
he is fluent, terribly fluent: he can express himself on any subject
(στωμύλος, λάλος, 91,841; *Ach.* 429, etc.). In manner too, he is conceited
and 'superior,' as the intellectual mostly seems to the low-brow. He
can not only speak himself, but he makes all his characters do so.

E. Next, I taught all the town to talk with freedom.
A.   I admit it.
 'Twere better, ere you taught them you had died amid their curses!
E. I gave them canons to apply and squares for making verses;
 Taught them to see, think, understand, to scheme for what they wanted,
 To fall in love, think evil, question all things. . . .
A.   Granted, granted!

This is still the intellectual criticized by the plain man. The intellectual applies canons of criticism; he also has a much wider range
of thought and discussion than the plain man thinks safe or proper or
even intelligible. He does teach his disciples to 'see, think, understand'
and perhaps also to 'question all things'—certainly Socrates did: and
is easily accused of teaching them to scheme, to give too much thought
to love, and to 'think evil.' This charge is made definite later on. Euripides has not only produced his Phaedras and Stheneboeas, he has
actually dared to introduce go-betweens on the tragic stage!

> What hasn't he done that is under the sun,
> And the love-dealing dames that with him have begun?
> One's her own brother's wife,
> One says 'Life is not Life,'
> And one goes into shrines to give birth to a son!
>
> (1078ff.)

The 'go-between' was perhaps the Nurse in the *Hippolytus;* in the
Aeolus, Macareus was in love with his sister Canacê; Augê the priestess,
ravished by Heracles, bore her child in the temple, praying Athena's
aid, and was cursed for her sacrilege. It is part of the joke that Aeschylus classes with these offences a thought which recurs in two beautiful passages of Euripides, that perhaps this life on earth is not our
true life.

> Who knoweth if the thing that we call Death
> Be life, and our life dying? Who knoweth?

Such sentiments may not be actually wicked, but they are all new-fangled and tiresome and wrong! They are the sort of thing that has actually made women commit suicide (1051)! Aeschylus claims that Euripides in this way has corrupted his generation:

Just think what they were when he had them from me!
  Good six-footers, solid of limb,
Well-born, well-bred, not ready to fly from obeying their country's call,
Nor in latter-day fashion to loiter and lie, and keep their consciences small.
Their life was in shafts of ash and of elm, in bright plumes fluttering wide,
In lance and greaves and corslet and helm, and hearts of seven-fold hide.

On which Dionysus—or according to some editors, Euripides—remarks:

Oh, now he's begun, and will probably run a whole armorer's shop on my
  head!

Was it really the solid six-footer, with no thought beyond his armor and the next battle, that made the greatest and best kind of Athenian? And did Aristophanes really think it was? A little later Aeschylus complains that Euripides and his like have taught

            the crews of the pick of the ships
To answer back pat to their officer's nose; how unlike my old sailor of yore,
With no thought in his head but to guzzle his brose, and sing as he bent at
  the oar!

Even that description scarcely suggests the highest type of Athenian sailor; but Dionysus adds other characteristics:

And drop dirt on the head of the rowers below, and garrotte stray lubbers
  ashore,
While our new man just sails where it happens to blow, and argues, and rows
  no more.

So evidently the old sailor was not in Aristophanes' eyes altogether an ideal type. (Cf. 965ff., 1039, on the respective pupils of the two poets.)

There is another criticism which is hard to estimate. The complaint sometimes takes the form that Euripides is too *terre à terre* and realistic. He himself claims that he has 'put things on the stage that came from daily life and business, where the audience could catch him if he tripped' (959ff.). His opponents, going further, say that his tragedies are full of beggar's staves, old hats, broken pots, and bottles without the cork, not to speak of 'the bed-quilt, or the oil-flask or the clothes-bag,' and make him wail, when these are taken from him, 'Man, you

have robbed me of my tragedy.' In the *Frogs* he claims, like Words-
worth, that he has simplified and clarified the language of tragedy,
which came to him swollen and feverish from the hands of Aeschylus.
Yet, at the same time, Aristophanes in scores of passages parodies not
the simplicity or prose-like quality of his diction, but its high-flown
tragic grandeur or its lyrical or romantic daring. The fact is that Euripides widened the whole range of tragedy. He made it more close
to life and clearer in expression, but also more romantic, adventurous,
and varied both in incident and in diction; and lastly he was a very
great lyric poet. The parodies show him now a realist, now a tragedian
of the pompous style, and now a peculiarly melodious and dreamy
singer. The very musicalness of his verse is made a charge against him.
The ancients, who were perhaps more sensitive than we to the psy-
chological effects of music, seem constantly, to associate subtlety and
melodiousness of rhythm with sensuality. Agathon's lyrics at the beginning of the *Thesmophoriazusae* are not only like 'the walking of
ants,' but are greeted by Mnesilochus with the exclamation:

> What melting words! And, as I heard them sung,
> Ye amorous powers, there crept upon my soul
> A pleasant dreamy raptuous titillation. (Rogers)

Yet there is not a word in them even remotely approaching the amorous. So in the *Frogs* (1327) a very musical and nonsensical parody of
Euripides, with some irregularities of meter but none of morals, reminds Aeschylus of the notorious 'dozen tricks' of the courtesan Cyrene,
and seems to demand the bones rather than the lyre for its accompaniment.

> Ye halcyons, by the dancing sea
> Who babble everlastingly,
>   While on your bathing pinions fall
> The dewy foam-sprays, fresh and free;
>   And Oh, ye spiders, deft to crawl
>   In many a chink of roof and wall,
> While left and right, before, behind,
> Your fingers wi-i-i-i-ind
>   The treasures of the laboring loom,
> Fruit of the shuttle's minstrel mind,
> Where many a songful dolphin trips
> To lead the dark-blue-beakèd ships,
> And tosses, with aërial touch,
> Temples and race-courses and such.
> O bright grape-tendril's essence pure,

> Wine to sweep care from human lips!
> Grant me, O Child, one arm-pressúre. . . .

At which point Aeschylus breaks off to denounce the metrical license of the last line. The verses certainly 'babble'; that is, they run trippingly and bewilderingly on into nonsense; the meter is slightly, very slightly, irregular; more serious in Aristophanes' eyes, the first syllable of εἱλίσσω, 'wind,' instead of having one musical note to itself, as in the strict old Greek music, is prolonged into a whole series of notes—a roulade. This does not suggest to our modern minds any grave undermining of morality. Nor does the parody of a Euripidean monody, or solo, which follows. It is too long to quote, but treats, with impassioned language and much variety of style, of the escape or theft of a cock from the singer's yard. She was suspecting no evil, but quietly wi-i-i-i-inding her wool, when

> He rose, rose in the air,
> On quivering blades of flight;
> He left me care, care,
> And tears, tears of despair,   ~
> Fell, fell, and dimmed my sight.

However, by the help of Hecate, Dictynna, and the Cretan Corybantes she hopes to recover him.

These are the best parodies in Aristophanes. They are really like Euripides, and have a touch of Euripidean loveliness in the midst of their absurdity, whereas the parodies of Aeschylus, which follow, are only strings of quotations incongruously put together. At any rate they enable us to see what Aristophanes criticized in the diction and the meter, though unfortunately not in the music. The incriminated music is lost to us, and we find it hard to understand how intensely the Greeks of this particular period felt about the changes of musical style which were then taking place.

It looks as if the whole matter were mostly one of convention and association. One might have expected, if our critic was bent on denouncing the moral atmosphere of Euripides, that he would attack his *Ionic a minore* lyrics, which, so far as meter goes, are clearly more sensuous and passionate than these simple glyconics. But no; the Ionic meters had been used by Aeschylus and Phrynichus, and Aristophanes merely found them 'as sweet as honey' (*Wasps*, 220). They were in the correct tragic tradition.

Only one of the tests to which the two poets are submitted brings out a clear result, the weighing of the verses. When all is said and done, the poetry of Aeschylus, verse by verse, weighs more and counts more. Euripides is eminently accomplished (σοφός). He has introduced numerous improvements into tragedy, he has removed many unskilfulnesses and flaws; he has made the range wider, the plots more ingenious, the characters more subtle and far more varied. He has made things articulate which in Aeschylus were confused and half-dumb. His Chorus, in place of the interminable discussions of theology with which Aeschylus occupied half the play, comes forward with lyrics in which the words themselves seem to sing and dance, and there is expression for every tone of emotion and every new invention of contemporary music. And yet, at the end of it all, he has made tragedy a smaller thing! The poetry of Aeschylus weighs more.

It is mere blundering to say that Aristophanes thinks Euripides a bad poet and Aeschylus a good, or that he hates the one and loves the other. He sees that both are great poets; he admires both, loves both, but at the end of the count, old Aeschylus, with the glow of Marathon still upon him, Aeschylus, who had triumphed with Miltiades and Aristîdes the Just, remains on his throne, shaken a little but not displaced. It is almost like comparing the regenerated Demos at the end of the *Knights* with the unregenerate Demos of Arginûsae; like comparing Aristîdes with Theramenes, the day of greatness with the day of downfall. And, apart from such associations, as a matter of pure art, the poetry of Aeschylus does really weigh more. He gives his vote for Aeschylus.

Yet, naturally enough, the verses that ran continually in his head, and seemed to weave about him a spell from which he had neither the power nor the desire to escape, were those of his own great contemporary.

The Literary Criticism of the *Frogs*

by G. M. A. Grube

Shortly after the death of Euripides, Aristophanes produced the *Frogs*. It is the most important critical document we possess from the fifth century, and probably the most amusing in the whole history of criticism. Dionysus, the god of tragedy, visits Heracles, who, as an old traveller to the underworld, may be able to give him useful hints; he explains that he has been reading the *Andromeda* and has decided to go down to Hades to fetch Euripides back, for he was a skillful poet (ποιητοῦ δεξιοῦ, 71). Heracles asks what's wrong with those now living, and they review them briefly. What of Iophon, the son of Sophocles? Well, he's the only good thing left but we cannot be sure yet. Why not fetch back Sophocles instead of Euripides? We'll just wait and see what Iophon is like on his own; besides, Euripides is such a clever rogue, he'll find ways to help in his escape, whereas Sophocles was always such an easy-going fellow.[1] Where's Agathon? He's left us to join the banquets of the blessed; a pity, he was a good poet and his friends miss him. Xenocles? Pythangelus?

> *Heracles:* Aren't there other little lads writing innumerable tragedies, more loquacious than Euripides by a mile?
>
> *Dionysus:* Yes, tiny grapes not worth the picking, mere chatterboxes; they produce one play, befoul tragedy once, and are never heard of again. You won't find a creative poet, look where you will.
>
> *Heracles:* How do you mean, creative?

"The Literary Criticism of the Frogs.*" From Chapter II, "Comedy: Aristophanes" in* The Greek and Roman Critics *by G. M. A. Grube (Toronto: University of Toronto Press, 1965; London: Methuen & Co., Ltd., 1965). Copyright © 1965 by G. M. A. Grube. Reprinted, with the reduction or elimination of footnotes, by permission of the author, the University of Toronto Press, and Methuen & Co., Ltd.*

[1] Sophocles died after Euripides, not long before the performance of the *Frogs*, and this is usually thought to account for the little notice which is taken of him in this play. Actually, however, three antagonists would have been awkward. In any case the contrast between Aeschylus as the representative of old Athens (he had died half a century before) and Euripides as the representative of the new is much clearer and more dramatic. Sophocles was not an easy butt of comedy, and references to him in the comedies are very few.

Dionysus: By creative I mean one who will venture some such bold phrase as 'Ether, halls of Zeus,' or 'the foot of time,' speak of a mind unwilling to take a sacred oath, the tongue having forsworn itself without the mind.
Heracles: You like these things?
Dionysus: I'm quite crazy about them.

Heracles thinks they're all nonsense, but as Dionysus rudely reminds him, he is hardly an expert: 'You teach me to eat.'

The whole scene makes clear that Aristophanes, who had ridiculed and satirized Euripides on the stage for over twenty years, fully recognized his genius and unhesitatingly classes him with Aeschylus and Sophocles as one of the three great tragedians of Athens. That verdict has never been disputed. We should note that in this scene there is no question of any moral judgment.

After a number of ludicrous adventures Dionysus has arrived in the underworld, and it is now suddenly discovered that a great contest is being prepared. In Hades every craft has its recognized master who dines at Pluto's table. Aeschylus was the master of tragedy, but Euripides, who has lately arrived, is terribly popular with all the knaves and rogues who make up the demos of the Underworld, and is challenging him for the Chair of Tragedy (τραγῳδικὸς θρόνος, 769). As for Sophocles, he reveres Aeschylus and will only enter the lists if Euripides should win. They were lacking a competent chairman, but who more appropriate than the god of tragedy, Dionysus himself?

So the great contest begins. It puts before us two different views of poetry and tragedy which are perennial and irreconcilable. True, the differences between the two tragedians are due, in part, to the difference of date. The tempo of Aeschylean tragedy was already archaic by 405 B.C. and so was a good deal of his language, while the rhetorical techniques of Euripides belong to the age of the sophists. Yet the plays of Aeschylus were still greatly admired and could be produced in competition with living dramatists, a privilege which, in 405, had been granted to no other dead poet. Essentially, however, the conflict goes much deeper, for it illustrates the opposition of the romantic idealist to the realist, the former believing that many true things are better ignored, the latter that the truth, the whole truth, is ultimately beneficial. This opposition extends to both matter, language, and style. The grand manner of Aeschylus requires dignified, stately language; the realism of Euripides inevitably uses everyday speech. It is part of Aristophanes' greatness that, in spite of all his prejudices in favor of Aeschylus, he could see the greatness and the attraction of both.

There is a preliminary skirmish (814-74), prayers and preparations

(875-904), a general engagement (905-1098), and then three separate assaults on specific points, namely the use of the *prologos* (1119-250), prosody and music (1251-363), and diction (1364-413).

The preliminary skirmish touches on points more fully debated later; it also contains Aeschylus' one witticism. He is, he says, at a disadvantage because his own plays survived him, while those of Euripides died with him and are therefore readily available in the Underworld!

The two contestants then each say a prayer. Aeschylus prays to Demeter, while Euripides invokes his new gods: Aether, the Twisting Tongue, and the Upturned Nose.

The first point of attack is the slow tempo and choral nature of Aeschylean tragedy. Some character, be it Achilles or Niobe, stands there veiled while the chorus sing a string of odes, and the audience wonder who it may be. Then, when the play is half over, he speaks a dozen tremendous words which no one understands. As for Euripides (939):

> When I took over from you our art, swollen with bombastic words and heavy phrases, I had to take some weight off her first and put her on a reducing diet of light verse, exercise and white beets, and give her chatter-juice strained from my books.

His characters, he goes on, name themselves right away; they do things from the first, and all of them talk—woman, slave, master, maiden, or old crone. 'That is the democratic way. I taught all of them to talk,' and they all know the techniques of talking. Their actions too are of an everyday sort which the audience understand, and so can check for themselves. But this is precisely what disgusts Aeschylus.

Euripides agrees that a poet should be admired 'for his skill, his advice, *and because we make men better*' (1009). This, says Aeschylus, is precisely what his own martial plays do, whereas Euripides, with his immoral plots, his Phaedras and Sthenoboeas, makes them a good deal worse. And here comes a famous passage (1052):

> *Euripides:* Do you mean that my story of Phaedra is untrue?
> *Aeschylus:* No by Zeus. It certainly is true, but the poet should veil depravity, not teach it by bringing it on the stage. *Children have school-masters to tell them, the poets are the teachers of men.* Therefore we should speak what is good.

Fine themes and fine words to suit them, that is the poet's function. And he mentions again Euripides' beggars in rags, the everlasting chattering and questioning which everybody apes nowadays instead of exercising in the gymnasium.

Up to this point Aeschylus' criticisms are based on moral grounds, while Euripides' are artistic, for even he could hardly attack the moral effect of Aeschylus' plays (perhaps the real Euripides might have done so, but Aristophanes certainly would not). Having agreed that poets are to be commended for poetic skill *and* moral teaching, Euripides has dealt with the former, Aeschylus with the latter.

From now on, however, we are mainly concerned with artistic criteria, and specific points.

First the *prologos,* i.e., that part of a tragedy which precedes the entrance of the chorus. Using the new methods of exegesis developed by the sophists, Euripides makes two charges against Aeschylus: obscurity and tautology, and proves them both. He shows that the first lines of the *Libation Bearers* can be interpreted in two different ways, and that there are two unnecessary words in three lines (1126). Aeschylus' counterattack is also twofold. The first point is trifling, namely that Euripides should not speak of 'once happy Oedipus,' for he was wretched from birth. The second is much more important, and its comic effect is shattering. He gets Euripides to quote the first lines of several plays and fits in the phrase 'and lost his oil-flask' within the first sentence, e.g. (1205),

Euripides: Aegyptus, as our common legends tell,
            Sailed with his fifty children o'er the seas,
            Arrived in Argos . . .
Aeschylus: . . . Lost his flask of oil.

The process is repeated half a dozen times, with any play Euripides cares to choose. The effect is very funny, but what does it mean? A Euripidean drama usually begins with a straight narrative to acquaint the audience with the story, or the particular version of it which the poet is adopting. Now in a straight narrative, neutral in emotional tone, a half line consisting of verb and object can before long be fitted in. The choice of the oil-flask, so common a piece of personal property in Greece, breaks the tragic dignity; it might just as well (as Aristophanes himself tells us at 1203) have been a blanket or a lunch kit. Aeschylus seems to mean that the Euripidean *prologos* stands outside the play and is in fact too much like a prologue in the modern sense, and also perhaps that the rhythm is monotonous, with frequent pauses in the middle of the third foot. This criticism, though it is often undeserved, has been repeated in almost every textbook.

The second specific criticism concerns the lyric meters of the two poets. Euripides criticizes the monotony of Aeschylean lyrics; they can almost be reduced to one and he reduces the major part of a number of lines to the last four-and-a-half feet of a Homeric hexameter.[2] Aeschylus replies by condemning modern variations in music and rhythm, of which he gives a number of examples from Euripides. The details are obscure but the main intention is clear. He then goes on to compose a parody of a Euripidean lyric monody. The meaning of this seems to be that the younger dramatist wastes great poetry on paltry subjects. 'A poor spinning girl lost her domestic cock and wishes to search the cottage of her neighbour Glyce whom she suspects of stealing it. That is all. But it is sung in strains that might befit a falling dynasty or some tremendous catastrophe of nations.' [3] Euripides here again is accused of debasing tragedy.

The third and last attack concerns the diction of the two poets, and it is judged by the comic device of bringing out scales and weighing the lines which the two adversaries throw into them. This is broad farce and the result is a foregone conclusion: the words of Aeschylus are the weightier. There was no need here for a serious judgment, only to point to the difference.

What is remarkable is that at the end of this prolonged contest Dionysus refuses to choose (1411):

> My friends, I am not going to judge between these men, for I don't want to be the enemy of either. I think the one so clever, and I like the other so.

With another abrupt change in the plot, Dionysus *now* tells us he came down to Hades to fetch the poet who would give the best advice to the city. After hearing them both, Dionysus still is unable to choose and finally decides on the basis of his own feelings only, and chooses Aeschylus.[4] Aristophanes could hardly have made it clearer that both are great poets, and that no choice is possible on aesthetic or artistic grounds. This is indeed a compliment to Euripides, after persecuting him on the stage for nearly a quarter of a century.

In this remarkable contest, which is the last critical scene in Aristophanes, it should be noted that both sides hit the mark and that, for all his prejudices in favor of Aeschylus, the comic poet is a remarkably impartial judge. Here and elsewhere he uses a number of

[2] This is the interpretation of Benjamin Rogers in his edition of the *Frogs*, xxv-xxix.

[3] *Ibid.*, xxiv.

[4] That the decision is not made on artistic grounds is clear from the passage just quoted. But, in spite of what many commentators say, it is not made on the grounds of the advice they give either, and this is more surprising, for here (i.e., as a teacher of men) one would have expected Aeschylus to win. . . . The decision is therefore explicitly subjective, it is based neither on poetic merit nor on moral-didactic grounds.

critical terms not previously used in our texts. Moral judgments are
intermingled with the artistic, but the two are not really confused.
As the critical ideas here dramatized are expected to be appreciated
by the audience, it is clear that they must have been topics of
conversation in Athens at the time.

Death and Life: The *Frogs*

by Cedric H. Whitman

The *Frogs* is by no means the first or only play built around a mission to the underworld in search of deceased worthies. In the *Demoi* of 412 Eupolis had resurrected a number of dead statesmen in order to set things right in Athens, and a few years later Aristophanes in the *Gerytades* appears to have done something similar, with an eye to recovering the poetry of the past. There is one fragment of Pherecrates in which Aeschylus, clearly in Hades, makes a boastful speech, and another in which a kind of Utopia in Hades is described. The theme is, in fact, related to that of Utopia, which was a favorite one with all the comic poets. Both Utopia and death are regions of the boundless, and though death is enclosed in a ring of darkness, it is nonetheless, as the ultimate receptacle of all good things, a kind of land of the heart's desire. In thinking of it, especially in anticipation of one's own death, it has not been customary to dwell upon the evils which also have found their way there, or to anticipate association with the damned. Death is, on this view, the land of departed goodness, and the comic convention of praising the past made it natural on occasion to stage the spirits of the great men of old amid the shadows of infernal landscapes.

It is doubtful, however, that either Eupolis or Pherecrates treated the journey into Hades in anything like the manner of Aristophanes. In the *Frogs* Hades is not only a Utopia; it also emerges as the land of truth, so to speak, the place where true values and true knowledge abide. When Dionysus has chosen Aeschylus rather than Euripides, the chorus sings (1482f.),

> Happy is the man who possesses
> Precise intelligence,

as though the god's choice had marked his arrival at something lastingly true. And of course it does: Dionysus had gone to Hades to recover the recently dead Euripides, the poet of the world of the present, but had become wiser during the journey and returned instead with the poet of Athens' early greatness. This action completes the explicit critique of tragedy which runs throughout the play; it also completes Dionysus' search for himself, which is equally, if not more, important.

It has recently been shown, in answer to attacks on the unity of the *Frogs,* that the play is carefully built around the development of Dionysus, who represents, in a complex way, the community of Athens, disjointed at first, but slowly re-achieving civic coherence through a journey into the unknown. The communal problem is only thinly masked as a poetic problem, for the two went hand in hand, with Euripides embodying the divisive and centrifugal forces of relativism, irresponsible rhetoric, and in general the new education, while Aeschylus stands for the staunch beliefs and public solidarity of the days of Marathon. The symbolic role of the two poets cannot be denied; what is rare is for Aristophanes to stage, in all seriousness, a character who represents, not the aspiring little individual, not the antisocial *poneros,* but the collective selfhood of Athens, a selfhood all but lost to its own identity and seeking to recover it by a spiritual journey into Hell. It is part of the immemorial heroic tradition for the questing individual to seek authenticity by a confrontation with death; by the loneliness of his search the hero does what all must do, and thus becomes Everyman. But Everyman is the universal individual. It is seldom that the heroic death journey can be conceived in terms of a community, for the community is, properly speaking, that which continues and outlives the individual. Yet that is what Dionysus is, Athenian culture incarnate, so to speak, undertaking the soul's far journey after self-knowledge and true identity. The club and lion-skin of Heracles are therefore not so wholly ludicrous as they at first appear, but make a kind of ironical disguise suggestive of an ulterior truth. In any case, the implications are highly complex, for somehow the question of communal continuity has been crossed with the myth of heroic self-search to make of Dionysus a character who bears a singularly heavy burden of meaning.

Dionysus' journey to Hades was not invented by Aristophanes. The story is told that the god, having established his cult throughout the known world, descended into the underworld in order to redeem not Euripides, but his mother Semele, whom he then brought to Olympus. Although the myth does not stand in any early author, Pindar seems to know of it, and it is likely that it is older than Aristophanes. It seems possible, at least, that the idea for the play had its origin in this story, for several of the details correspond. It is said that the god did not know the way to Hades, and had to ask it of a certain Prosymnus; in Aristophanes, this aspect of the journey has become the prologue with Heracles, whom Dionysus consults about (112f.)

> havens, bakeries,
> Brothels, rest areas, detours, fountains, roads,
> Towns, buildings, hostesses of inns with fewest
> Bedbugs.

Usually Dionysus is said to have descended through the Bottomless Lake of Lerna. Another version has it that he went down through a great chasm at Troezen; this place, according to Plutarch, was called the Place of Forgetfulness. The name may possibly account for the Plain of Lethe which Charon lists among the places whither his skiff is about to sail. In any event, it seems clear that the scenario of the *Frogs* is built upon the legend of Dionysus' quest for his mother, and that the themes of life, death, and immortality, so prevalent in the play, have their roots in this apocalyptic myth of resurrection and apotheosis.

Mythic tradition may also account for certain other details, and even for the chorus of the play, consisting as it does of the redeemed souls of the Eleusinian initiates. Once more, it is hard to say how early the story was invented, but Dionysus is said to have been initiated into the Mysteries before he went down to Hades, and so too was Heracles. One of the benefits promised by the Mysteries was some kind of return from the nether darkness. The two brothers of the prologue are, therefore, the only two gods who had ever been initiated into the Mysteries, and Heracles had been initiated as a mortal, before he was taken up into Olympus. As for Dionysus, it is a tormented question to what extent, if at all, he was associated with the Mysteries of Demeter; but he was surely by the middle of the fifth century identified with the Eleusinian Iacchus, the divine personification of the exultant, mystic procession. The point need not be labored; but Dionysus appears in the play not only as the god of the theater, but also as a deity affiliated, if only by initiation, with the Eleusinian Mysteries, and therefore with one of the greatest of Athenian cults and the only one which dealt specifically with the eschatological fortunes of the soul. The chorus of Mystae which greets Dionysus in Hades is a collective representation of an Athens redeemed beyond the grave, and if the god does not recognize himself in the invocation of Iacchus, he nonetheless is moved to join in the dancing and singing. This whole aspect of the play could be regarded as a montage upon the initiation of Dionysus, who, like any initiate, is in search of his own and his city's salvation; the old myth is transposed into a comic mode, yet retains its basic meaning.

But the montage is a multiple one. The principal scene of the play is, of course, the agon between Euripides and Aeschylus, so that the dramatic contests of the City Dionysia are also adumbrated. B. B. Rogers long ago noted that the boat fare which Charon collects is not one obol, the usual charge for conveyance across the Styx, but two, which is the entrance fee for the theater. The *Frogs* thus becomes a play within a play, the first known example in Western literature of that haunting device which was to become a total theatrical method with Pirandello. The mode is apt for artistic self-scrutiny, for thus the poet holds the mirror, not up to life, but up to another mirror, as it were, thus producing an infinite regress of implication. One is not sure whether he is saying that the world is a stage or that the stage is the world, and this ambiguity is carried out in the more searching one of life and death. Since the demise of Euripides and Sophocles the price of a theater ticket has become the price of entering the realm of the dead, and there alone can a "fruitful," "generative" poet be found. Only on the initiates in Hades do the sun and gay light shine.

Imagery drawn from the theater is ubiquitous throughout, and nothing could be more subtle than the way in which the question of Dionysus' identity is developed through the critique of dramatic poetry; for if the second half of the play explicitly (though not necessarily too scientifically) explores the nature of tragedy, the first half weighs the nature of comedy. As patron of both arts Dionysus may appropriately seek to know himself by knowing them. The very opening lines of the play set the tone of self-conscious artistry:

> *Xan.:* Shall I say one of the usual things, master,
> The sort of thing the audience always laughs at?

Bantering the audience was a frequent part of Old Comedy, but this jibe leads to something more. Dionysus' reply indicates a certain discrimination about kinds of humor, and he forbids certain jokes which, he says, make him feel a year older—the very opposite of the rejuvenation motif so frequently observed in comedy. Before a dozen lines have passed, however, two of the prohibited jests—dull vulgarities, fit only for Aristophanes' rivals—are trundled out, and something very like a third occurs somewhat later. Clearly the art of comedy is out of hand, if its own deity has so little control of it; and presently, as he arrives at Heracles' door, the question of what he is up to arises quite directly.

Whatever was said earlier about the possible appropriateness of some of Dionysus' equipment, the combination of club, lion-skin, tragic buskin, and a woman's robe is a strangely assorted one, and the astonishment of Heracles is understandable enough. Piling as it does male, female, and animal disguises on the person of a god, the costume

may fairly be described as grotesque; almost as if to complete the
hybrid picture, the god is several times referred to as a "man." But the
grotesquerie has a different significance from that of Peithetaerus:
Dionysus is a hybrid whose multiple guises indicate not the possession
of secret and magical keys, but rather uncertainty as to who he is. It
is as if the theater were enacting all its repertoire at once in a self
burlesque. Yet this farrago, which cannot choose but be hilarious, is
composed of things which hint at tragic and heroic seriousness; even
the woman's robe is no exception. For though by the fifth century
Dionysus was often represented as an effeminate youth, the female
dress (κροκωτός) can hardly fail to recall specifically its counterpart
in the dress of Agathon in the *Thesmophoriazusae*, and the symbolism
thereof, noted earlier. Aristophanes has costumed his main character
admirably to his purpose: in the light of the deaths of Sophocles and
Euripides, comedy puts on the buskin of high seriousness and the club
and lion-skin of heroic self-search, and undertakes the quest to recover
poetic and political virility. Perhaps for this reason the word which
Dionysus chooses for the kind of poet he wants is γόνιμος, literally
"fruitful," "generative," a word expressive of natural, healthy fertility.
Dionysus thinks that Euripides is such a poet, but his view changes
once his own real identity is established in Hades.

The question of identity is dramatized with full comic effect in the
middle scenes of the play. Since these scenes have been carefully analyzed of late, be it said but briefly that Dionysus, though he has
claimed that he could "play Ercles rarely," does not in fact live up to
the fiercer part of his costume when faced with characters whom
Heracles mistreated on his trip into Hell. Aeacus, still seething over
the rape of Cerberus, bursts out in a thunderous salvo of threats, and
the terrified god promptly induces Xanthias to exchange his burden of
luggage for the club and lion-skin. The process is quickly reversed, however, when a maid enters with an invitation for Heracles to dinner,
complete with roast ox, cake, and dancing girls. But as Dionysus-
Heracles is about to enjoy these pleasures, he is assailed by the hostess
of an inn whose goods Heracles formerly had devoured without paying.
The costumes are changed again, so that when Aeacus returns with
bailiffs and constables, it is Xanthias the slave whom he points out
as the thief of Cerberus. The theatrical imagery is never forgotten: a
shift of costumes is a shift of roles, and therefore a shifting of responsi-
bility. But in the ordeal which follows the ground too shifts a little.
Xanthias maintains his role of Heracles, but denies the charges against
him, and offers his "slave" for torture to prove his innocence. Dionysus,
cornered, tells his real name, and to settle the dispute, it is agreed that
whichever cannot feel the blows of a whip is the real god. The question

is now not which is Heracles, but which is a god and which the slave. The elimination of the Heracles disguise brings Dionysus one step further toward his true self, but the ordeal is inconclusive, and Aeacus refers the matter to Pluto and Persephone, by whom it is promptly settled offstage during the parabasis.

The repeated interchanges of slave and free man, or at least slave and god, glance at the manumission of the slaves who fought at Arginusae. Xanthias had not fought, but he shows some of the stamina necessary for putting himself on an equal basis with the free. Loaded with bundles, he cries to Dionysus (33f.):

> What a wretch am I! Why didn't I fight at sea?
> Then I'd have given you something to howl about.

In turning the tables on Dionysus he shows some genuine *poneria*, though it is less the *poneria* of the comic hero, than of the clever slave of New Comedy. His general superiority to his master is made clear throughout the first part of the play, especially in the recurrence of words meaning "noble" or "gentleman." For lack of a porter Xanthias agrees to go on carrying the bundles; "You are noble and a gentleman," says Dionysus by way of thanks. Aeacus likewise finds Xanthias a man of proper breeding (179; 640). When the truth comes out, however, it is Dionysus who Aeacus has decided is the true gentleman; but Xanthias quickly undercuts his judgment with the remark "What else should he be but a gentleman, who knows nothing but drinking and lechery?" (739f.)

The question of free men versus slaves becomes explicit in the famous parabasis, sometimes thought to be one of the clearest examples of political programming in Aristophanes; deeply felt as the passage is, there is no program, but only a yearning for a real Athens and real Athenians. Aristophanes writes in a prescriptive mode, appropriate to the role of comic "educator" (693f.):

> So I say it's villainous that those who fought one fight at sea
> All are now reborn Plataeans, slaves no longer, masters, free;
> Yet, I can't say this was badly done, but rather to be classed
> With the most intelligent resolutions that you've ever passed.
> Others though, your brothers, men who manned your fleet,
>   their fathers too,
> Wisely banish wrath, forgive one fault, and take them back to you!
> Let all men be kept our kinsmen, citizens, enfranchised free,
> One condition still availing—tug an oar and fight at sea!

These lines urging, as they seem to do, common sense and a general amnesty for those involved in the revolution of 411, are echoed in the corresponding epirrheme by words of more general import. In a fine image comparing citizens, new and old, with the currency of Athens, now badly debased, Aristophanes calls upon the city to make use of its good citizens, and he pours out all the words implying civic righteousness—

καλὸς κἀγαθός, εὐγενής, σώφρων, δίκαιος, χρηστός,
("noble," "well-born," "moderate," "just," "upright")

—to describe the men "reared in gymnasium, dances, and music." But the supply of these is low, and when later Aeschylus asks if Athens employs her good citizens, Dionysus must reply that she does not, but rather employs the wicked perforce, for lack of better. It appears thus from the parabasis that parallel with the search for a great poet runs the search for the good citizen, and that these two searches are in no way distinct from Dionysus' search for his true selfhood; they constitute in great part its meaning, as is clear from much of the great agon. But throughout the multiple changes of role, in the first part of the play it seems unlikely that the quest will be fulfilled, and Dionysus' final reply to Aeschylus about good citizens is not very encouraging.

The confusion between slave and free reaches a rather weird climax in the intermediate scene just after the parabasis. It is now clear who Dionysus is, and that Xanthias is the slave; but so too, it turns out, is Aeacus himself, and the two compare notes on the low satisfactions of slavery—privately cursing the master, spying on his secrets, telling them abroad, and so on. All these little joys constitute a special world, presided over by a new and unfamiliar aspect of Zeus himself: Xanthias speaks of "brother Zeus," and, "Zeus who is our fellow whipping post" (750; 756). Even the Eleusinian aspect is included: Aeacus so delights in slavish knavery that it seems to initiate him into "Final Revelation," and he uses the verb denoting the last stage of the Mysteries (745). To each his own; the true levels are emerging. The recognition of Dionysus by Pluto could scarcely have been made good comic material; instead, Aristophanes stages the parallel unmasking of Xanthias, but to keep the unlikelihood of it all alive, he turns Aeacus too into a slave. And not only Aeacus, the divine judge of the dead, but also Zeus has been transformed into a slave, to complete the inverted image of a society where nothing is any longer what it is supposed to be. The scene forms a skillful transition between the role-changing of the first part of the play and the slow discovery of the true poet in the second.

The shifting of roles between Dionysus and Xanthias, however, is only part of a larger scheme, deeply basic to the play. It was said above that the god is in search of something lastingly true; but before he approaches it he is driven through phase upon phase of seeming and

changeability, of which his own transformations are a reflection. The
scene with Empusa is like a motif (288f.):

Xanth.: By Zeus, I see a monster, very big!
Dion.: What sort?
Xanth.:   Dreadful. It turns all kinds of things,
Sometimes a cow, sometimes a mule, sometimes
A beautiful woman.
Dion.:   Where is she? Let me at her!
Xanth.: It's not a woman any more, but hound.
Dion.: Ah, it's Empusa!
Xanth.:   Yes, and her whole face
Is alight with fire.
Dion.:   And has she one brass foot?
Xanth.: Yes, by Poseidon, and the other—dung!

Faced with this shifty apparition, Dionysus in terror forbids his servant
to address him either as Heracles or by his right name, thus rejecting
identity altogether. Well may he do so in a world where good citizens
languish in exile, while slaves overnight turn into "Plataeans and masters" (694). The chorus ironically praises, later, the kind of adaptability
which keeps a man out of trouble (534f.):

This is the way of a man of brains
And shrewdness, one who has been around:
To turn himself forever about,
To whatever side is the fortunate side,
Rather than stand like a painted picture,
With only one device. To shift
To the cozier berth is the way of the man
Who is bright and, by nature, Theramenes.

Theramenes had already become, justly or unjustly, a byword for self-
interested fence-jumping, and had perhaps also earned his famous nick-
name, cothurnus, the boot which fits either foot; if so, there is doubtless yet a further significance in that part of Dionysus' costume. He is
god not only of roles, but of shifting roles, in a monstrous Empusa-
world where nothing is stable, and everything turns into something
else; even comedy is turning into tragedy.

In the latter half of the play the theme of changeability deepens and
begins to involve the whole question of relativism. We have seen in
the *Birds* a lofty extravaganza upon the relative or subjective nature
of reality, and the demiurgic power of speech; indeed, much of the
earlier work of Aristophanes showed a tendency to exploit this sophistic theory, while overtly condemning it with mock-moral zeal. But the

Frogs is different. Here, instead of contenting himself with the language of absurdity and the salvation of private reality, Aristophanes seems to be trying to plunge deeper, to get beyond the veils of speech, and arrive at something more absolute. Speech is no longer the touchstone of personal power over the world; it has become the symbol of individual deception, disintegration of reality, and social decay. Euripides appears as the embodiment of talk, both trivial and shifty, a quibbling immoralist concerned on the one hand with verbal exactitude, and on the other with morally ruinous equivocation. The role is no new one for him, of course, but there is a contrast between the negative function it fulfills here and that which it served in the *Acharnians,* where the rhetoric of Euripides provided the tool for a heroic success. Here, it seems, Euripides is to blame for all the ills of society (1069f.):

Aesch.: What next? You taught them to practice babble and insubordinate
     mouthing!
     The result of your teaching was empty gymnasia, thin buttocks worn
     to a frazzle,
     As the boys went yammering on and on; and the men of the fleet you
     persuaded
     To answer their officers back! But I, in the old days, when I was
     living,
     They knew no more than to shout for a loaf, and call "heave-ho, my
     hearties!"

And not only has he corrupted the fleet; on account of his plays, which presented procurers, childbirths in temples, incestuous siblings, and people "saying life isn't life," the whole city is "full of undersecretaries, political buffoons, and deceivers" (1078f.). This is no mean accomplishment for a dramatic poet, to be personally responsible for the demagogues and bureaucracy. But it is all because, unlike Aeschylus, he had made all the characters in his plays *talk* (948f.):

Eurip.: Well then, from the very first I wasted no opportunity, not I!
     With me the women talked, no less the slave talked, and the master
     Talked, and the young girl talked, the old woman talked . . .
Aesch.:   You should have been murdered.

Once more, it is worth noting how Aristophanes slips back and forth between the context of the theater and real life. Euripides' characters talk glibly and so do the Athenians; the poet, however, is not represented as reflecting society but impelling it, according to the conventional view of antiquity that the poet educates the people, and it is his task to improve his fellow citizens. Euripides' prize pupil, however, is Theramenes, the slippery politician mentioned earlier by the chorus

as more remarkable for versatility and self-preservation than for stead-
fastness of principle. And the result of all his teaching is a world of
vain and garrulous argument, limitless questioning, insubordination,
and pusillanimous suspicion.

In contrast with all this talk is the silence of Aeschylus. Upon his
first entrance Aeschylus disdains to speak at all in reply to the vitupera-
tions of his rival. Euripides accuses him of putting on airs, just as he
did in his tragedies; indeed, the first fault that Euripides finds with
Aeschylus is that his characters did not talk enough (911f.):

Eur.: Well, first he'd sit one character down, all muffled up in mourning,
  Achilles, say, or Niobe, not even their faces showing—
  A poor excuse for tragedy—and never a grunt or murmur.
Dion.: That's true by Zeus!
Eur.:   The chorus, though, would pile up strings of lyric,
  Four odes straight off without a break; and they just sat in silence.

Half the play went by before anyone but the chorus said anything, and
then out would come twelve words, the size of bulls, which nobody
could understand. However adroit the satire, we are bound to prefer
Aeschylus' long silence and twelve big words to the prattle of Euripides
not only by the final outcome, but also by the prayers uttered by the
two poets before the contest begins. Aeschylus, an Eleusinian by birth,
prays solemnly (886f.):

  Demeter, you who nurtured up my mind
  Let me be worthy of your Mysteries.

It should be remembered that the climactic vision of the Mysteries was
protected by a vow of silence, a secrecy so strict that to this day we
know nothing of the *epopteia*. Euripides, however, prays to his own
private gods, a "new coinage," as Dionysus says, recalling the imagery
of the parabasis, where the new, worthless citizens are compared to the
debased currency of the war years (892f.):

  Ether, my fodder, and axle of the tongue,
  Intelligence, and nostrils of keen scent,
  Let me refute what words I meet withal.

Though the language of both poets is subjected to the most scorching
parody, "horse-crested and plank-sized" words versus "splinters and
filings," at root it is the contest between the axle of the tongue and the
holy silence of Demeter, the contrived ambiguities of speech versus that
which is always true.

Near the end of the agon the matter is treated more explicitly, and
also in darker colors. Dionysus is weighing individual lines in a scale.

This scene, itself a parody of an epic *psychostasis*, or weighing of lives to see which will die and which will live, has somewhat deathly overtones, and the image of death supplants that of silence. Euripides offers a line from his *Antigone* (1391f.):

> Eur.:   Persuasion has no shrine other than speech.
> Aesch.: Alone of gods Death has no love for gifts.
> Dion.: Let go, let go; again, he's heavier.
>   He threw in Death, a very weighty ill.
> Eur.:   But I threw in Persuasion, a fine word.
> Dion.: Persuasion's light and empty, and makes no sense.

Persuasion, *Peitho*, is explicitly rejected; the mainspring of the *Birds* and of so many other plays, the comic touchstone, the almighty word, is swept away by death. A few lines later Aeschylus does it again; he outweighs a huge mace with two corpses. Comedy yields to tragedy, and the kaleidoscopic multiplicity of speech yields to the single, ineluctable fact of death.

It had always been Aristophanes' way to revel in the multifariousness of things. The hero's will to the boundless carried with it the power to transform everything to advantage, and all these self-interested transformations lie close to the heart of comic poetry. The comic hero identifies with the boundless, becoming what he will in it, untroubled by considerations of consistency. The tragic hero's relation with the boundless differs somewhat; he confronts it, or enters it, but rather than identifying with it, he extracts something from it, a single truth. And it is this which Dionysus is doing in the *Frogs*. He seeks to extract from the boundless world of death the true poet, and to do so he must penetrate and pass beyond the infinite shiftingness and changeability of the phenomenal world, transcend the Many and find the One. Euripides is found to be the dramatist of words, and his buskin is that of Theramenes; he is the poet of the Many. Dionysus was intent on bringing him back, but he himself lacked true identity, and had to keep changing costumes. In the lyrical competition Aeschylus again drives home the all too diverse nature of his opponent's poetry, and damns it as meretricious; he himself derived his lyrics from the "fair source for a fair purpose," presumably meaning Homer, but Euripides got his from all kinds of sources indiscriminately (1301f.):

> Aesch.: He draws his songs from everything, from harlots,
>   Meletus' drinking catches, Carian flutings,
>   Dirges, and dance music.

His very variety is against him, and Aeschylus proceeds to give a sample of Euripidean lyric, which he compares to the versatility of the cour-

tesan Cyrene, famous for no less than twelve different modes of sexual
intercourse. Cyrene climaxes Aeschylus' strictures upon Euripides'
plays about sexual problems as Theramenes climaxes the charges of
glib speech and political instability; but both represent the variety
which is devoid of a central core, the diversity which is the opposite
of truth.

When Dionysus finally chooses Aeschylus, he disposes of Euripides
with three of his own equivocations. The first of these states clearly the
lubricity of speech (1469f.):

> *Eur.:* Remember now the gods by whom you swore
> To bring me home again! Choose now your own.
> *Dion.:* "My tongue swore"; and my choice is Aeschylus.

The famous line (612) from the *Hippolytus,* "My tongue swore but not
my heart," liberates Dionysus, and the poet of verbal equivocation is
caught in his own trap. In the second equivocation moral relativism
destroys itself (1474f.):

> *Eur.:* Can you look me in the face, having wrought such shame?
> *Dion.:* What's shame, unless it seem so to the audience?

The parody here serves a double purpose. Euripides had written,
"What is shame, unless it seem so to the person who commits it?"
Dionysus not only makes use of Euripides' own dismissal of exterior or
objective moral standards, but in substituting "the audience" he rein-
vokes the theatrical imagery of the play, with its tone of conscious
dramatic self-criticism, and implies that the audience will not think it
a shame at all to leave Euripides in Hell. The third equivocation will
be taken up later.

But to answer the multiformity of language with the uniformity of
silence, or perhaps of death, is scarcely to resolve the poetic or political
problem. There is another and more positive alternative to the decep-
tiveness of speech, and that is music. But it must be true music; that
of Euripides will not do, of course. When Aeschylus is about to give his
parody of Euripidean lyric, he sets aside the lyre, calling instead for an
accompaniment of castanets, the instrument of dancing girls and
treated elsewhere in a comic fragment as typical of mere noise. The art
of Euripides, composed of "debates, and twists, and turns," leads to
chaos, and is attractive principally to "highwaymen, cutpurses, parri-
cides, and housebreakers." True music is explicitly contrasted by the
chorus with the quibblings of philosophy (1491f.):

> Go, cast off music, poetry,
> And sit with Socrates and gas!

> Leave the great art of tragedy
> And be—an ass!
>
> Go, plunge in solemn argument,
> And spend a worthless afternoon
> In quibble, quiddity and cant,
> And be—a goon!

True music, the great art of tragedy, was what Dionysus went to Hades to rescue, "that the city might be saved and present her choruses" (1419). True music reflects and encourages cultural cohesiveness; it includes, by implication in the symbolic scheme, both a public and a private moral force which penetrates and illuminates society.

Ironically, this ethical theory of music seems to have been first formulated by the sophist Damon, the pupil of Prodicus, much admired by Socrates and Plato; but it is by no means untypical of Aristophanes to assume and exploit a principle which he would not tolerate if theoretically expounded. Yet there is reason herein, for theoretical formulation from one point of view embarrasses the intuition of music's cultural power; analysis is a kind of talk, and by its basic definition it dissolves the economy of symbols and confounds their effect. In any case, Aristophanes is dealing not in theory but example, and he has staged the cultural cohesiveness of Athens, not only in the symbolic figure of Aeschylus, but also in the chorus of Mystae with their lovely hymns of mingled revelry and reverence. As suggested above, the Eleusinian aspects of the *Frogs* indicate an Athens redeemed from time, suffering, and error, albeit on the other side of the veil. The music of the Mystae is emphasized: "Thereafter, the breath of flutes will surround you," says Heracles to Dionysus; and presently, after the Empusa episode, the flutes are heard (154; 313).

The Mystae are unusually friendly for a comic chorus, which has a tendency to enter in warlike mood; but this is inevitable in view of their character as spirits of harmony and gentle piety. Like the chorus of birds, they sing in pastoral images, invoking the gods, celebrating the beauties of nature. But there is no irony here; nature is purified in the simplicities of singing, play, and sacred dance (372f.):

> Go forward now, each manfully,
> On to the flowering folds
> Of the meadows,
> Dancing and mocking, playing and jesting:
> Our feast was full enough!
>
> But come, that you may worthily
> Exalt the goddess of salvation,

Chanting aloud to her who promises
To save this land forever.

The invocation of Kore as goddess of salvation obviously strikes the
central theme of the play, and is echoed by the prayer to Demeter to
"preserve her own chorus, to play and dance all day in safety" (388f.).
In these prayers one hears the twinge of real anxiety for the city, perhaps a specific reference to the suspension of the Eleusinian proces-
sions because of the besieging Spartans. But these songs are also part
of the music of a sound and healthy city, a city of men "nourished in
palaestras, choral dances, and music" (729). It is a mystical music in
every sense, as the chorus all but states, calling upon the "Muse of the
sacred chorus," and referring to the rites of Demeter and of the Muses
by the same word, *orgia*, connoting secret enactments or mysteries
(675). True music and the redeeming Mysteries are one, and the cory-
phacus, acting as hierophant in the parabasis-like passage which inter-
rupts the lyrics of the parodos, specifically excludes from the ceremonies not only malefactors against the city, but also "whoever has
never seen the *orgia* of the noble Muses, nor danced, nor been initiated
into the mysteries of the tongue of bull-eating Cratinus" (356f.).

Not the least musical element in the play is the little extra chorus of
frogs. What they are doing in the play, and why they should give it its
title, are questions not easy to answer. Charon, however, speaks of
them in something of the way that Heracles speaks of the beautiful
light and the flute music of the Mystae (202f.):

> *Charon:* Will you stop babbling and brace your feet
>   And row with zeal?
> *Dion.:*   And how ever should I,
>   Unskilled, unoceaned, and unsalamised,
>   How should I row?
> *Charon:*   Easily. You will hear songs,
>   Most lovely, if you once lay to.
> *Dion.:*   What sort?
> *Charon:* Wonderful. Swan-frogs.

Swans are sacred to Apollo, and for some reason have always been
thought of as possessed of the power of song, albeit only at the hour
of death. These ghostly swan-frogs have something of the magical
hybrid about them, and their compelling rhythm has its effect on
Dionysus; they are, after all, his own frogs (211f.):

> Offspring of lakes and fountains we,
> Sing we the cry that rings in concord

With hymns, my clear-voiced song,
  Koax, koax,
The song that once we shouted aloud
Round Dionysus, son of Zeus,
In Limnae, when on the Feast of Pots
The drunken-headed rout of the people
Came to my sacred precinct,
  Brekekekex, koax.

Dionysus finds rowing painful and the song monotonous. A strange
interchange follows (221f.):

> *Dion.:* I'm getting a pain in the tail, *koax.*
>   That, I suppose, means nothing to you.
> *Frogs:* *Brekekekex-koax-koax!*
> *Dion.:* To hell with you and your *koax!*
>   There's nothing to you but *koax!*
> *Frogs:*   Of course, O Busybody!
>   For I am loved by the Muses of the lovely lyre,
>   By horned Pan who plays the vocal reed pipe,
>   And Apollo the harper, too, takes joy in me.

Do Apollo, the Muses, and Pan particularly love monotonous music?
Perhaps we have here no more than a frog's-eye view of aesthetics, but
the song does not, at least, suffer from the indiscriminate and slatternly
multiformity of Euripides.

Moreover, these frogs are associated with the spring festival of Dionysus in Limnae, the Anthesteria, not with strange deities like Ether or
the axle of the tongue. They are genuine Athenian frogs, and above all,
they teach Dionysus to row, whereas the sailors brought up on Euripides
are good only at talking back to their officers. The rhythm of the frogs
is the rhythm of the victorious Athenian fleets, and Dionysus learns it
despite himself, to the sorrow of his blistered hands and backside. He
begs them to stop, but the frogs croak on and on, urging each other to
sing, as the Mystae also do, until the god takes up the song himself
and finally shouts them down. The episode is one of Aristophanes' most
graceful and droll inspirations, and though it may seem at first to have
little connection with the rest of the play, it is in fact closely bound to
it by the theme of music, true and false, and it forms a legitimate part
of the quest for the "generative" poet and the sound citizen. With their
animal grumpings and unchanging refrain, they balance grotesquely
the sublime invocations of the immortal Mystae, and the verb which
they use of their own singing, ἰαχέω, is that which was used to describe
the religious shouting of the initiates in procession.

Interspersed with the imagery of music, run occasional images of light and darkness, corresponding vaguely to salvation and damnation. The Hell of Mud, described by Heracles, where sinners (including admirers of Morsimus) wallow, and the "darkness and filth" reported by Xanthias are probably not derived specifically from anything in Eleusinian ritual, though they may be Orphic. The light, however, is certainly Eleusinian, for it is at first simply the light of the torch procession, described in advance by Heracles and presented on stage in the parodos. Iacchus is invoked as the "dawn star of the nightly initiation," holding a torch, and the whole meadow gleams with the flare (340f.). At the end of the parodos the light of the actual torches begins to blend into the supernal joyous light of that other sun which shines "only on the initiates who have kept their lives holy" (455f.). The lines are reminiscent of Pindar's descriptions of the afterlife of the blest, and presumably represent the kind of bright future promised by the Mysteries to the initiates.

The Eleusinian torch is the lamp of redemption, and it has cultural implications within the play, as well as personal, eschatological ones. Aeschylus, as we have observed, is closely associated with the cluster of Eleusinian images and themes throughout. He is even addressed by the same epithet as Iacchus and Kore. As he finishes his first denunciation of Euripides, describing the social corruption resulting from the unhappy poet's work, he adds (1087f.):

> Now, all through a lack of manly training,
> There is no one left who can lift a torch.

The image is there, though this torch may be not an Eleusinian one specifically; Dionysus, agreeing, takes it as a Panathenaic one (1089f.):

> By Zeus, there isn't! I almost withered
> With laughing, at the Panathenaea,
> When some slow fellow ran, all bent over,
> Pale-skinned and fat, lagging behind,
> And fussing along; and the potters that stood
> At the gates all whacked him,
> Belly and buttock and flank and rib,
> Till what with the flats of their palms, well smacked,
>   With a bit of a fart,
> He blew out his lamp and escaped.

Panathenaic or Eleusinian, the torch is a property of a city festival, a token of its cultural integrity, and Euripides' man blows it out. Aeschylus, however, as he returns "to the light" to save the city, is escorted by the sacred lamps of the Mystae to music of his own composing. The true light and the true music join at the end in the vision of salvation.

Before attempting to penetrate the meaning of that vision, and the selection of Aeschylus as its minister, it may be well to re-emphasize the symbolic nature of the two poets as presented. The agon is often taken for essentially serious literary criticism, but if the foregoing analysis of the imagery is in any sense correct, it is clear that the whole literary level is ancillary to a larger design, in which the survival of Athens forms the core. Poets are, as a rule, representative of their times, and it was logical to let Aeschylus speak for the glorious Athenian past, and Euripides for the contemporary decay. To cast the conflict in the form of a literary debate was a scheme which offered infinite opportunity for parody and caricature. The Euripides here presented, however, is much the same straw figure that appeared in the *Acharnians* and *Thesmophoriazusae,* and the Aeschylus who thunders about in images of storms and wild beasts is only his antitype, carefully contrived to knock him down. Caricature, to be effective, must include some truth, and doubtless there is some truth in these, but it can hardly be called serious literary criticism to let these two inventions sneer at each other for seven hundred lines, or to equate the art of Aeschylus with obscurity and bombast, and that of Euripides with the harlot Cyrene. It is sometimes said, also, that Aristophanes is quite impartial in his distribution of the blows exchanged by the two tragedians, but this is not really true; Euripides lands a few adroit punches, but the cards are stacked in Aeschylus' favor from the very first, when Dionysus addresses him as "Most-honored Aeschylus," the epithet of Iacchus, and says in the next line, "wicked (*poneros*) Euripides" (851f.). The agon is constructed in five parts, devoted respectively to the criticism of plots and purpose, prologues, lyrics, poetic "weight," and practical advice. In all five Aeschylus is the second speaker, with the advantage of the climactic last word. No real concern is felt for the justice of either's claims: it is not true that Aeschylus always wrote about wars and Euripides always wrote about sex; Aeschylus' choruses are seldom really obscure, and Euripides' seldom, if ever, trivial; and one scholar, at least, has shown that the trick of "ruining prologues with one small oil flask" can be used, not only on Aeschylus, but even on the immaculate style of Sophocles himself. Parody exists for fun's sake, and there is plenty of fun here.

But if serious literary criticism is lacking, especially in regard to the actual details discussed, that does not mean that there is no serious level in the agon. It is, literally, a life-and-death struggle, dramatized in terms of literature. Whatever be the case for the poet as pedagogue, Aristophanes has, by association, made his two poets into composite

symbols, each of a condition or state of affairs in the Athenian com-
monwealth, one spelling life and the other death. We have seen, in
the first part of the agon, how Aeschylus' grand and martial themes
bred a generation of soldiers with the virile virtues of Patrocluses and
Teucers, while the domestic intrigues of Euripides were responsible
for the bureaucrats and Theramenes. The next section, on prologues,
has the fewest symbolic overtones, if any. But by the end of the battle
of the lyrics Euripides has been neatly packaged up with Cyrene, and
associated with infinite variability and lack of authenticity. With the
weighing of lines the colors really darken as the grim reality of death
sweeps away *Peitho,* and the delusiveness of speech. At this point the
fact that Dionysus says that he is unable to decide between the two
does not mean that Aristophanes cannot; it is simply that the tension
must be maintained through the last part of the agon, the contest in
practical advice, where all the cards are finally laid on the table, and
the full tragedy of the situation is delicately but firmly made clear.
Aeschylus is, of course, chosen; but what does that mean?

To a poet of the Old Comedy all things were possible, and we are
therefore perhaps at liberty to think that Aristophanes, in resurrecting
Aeschylus, is simply bringing back the good old days with as gay a
disregard for the facts of life as when Dicaeopolis made his private
treaty with Sparta. But the atmosphere of the *Frogs* is against this
view; a real fear for the city is felt throughout, implicit in the various
references, at once proud and anxious, to the recent sea fight off
Arginusae; explicit in such remarks as the city lying "in the arms of
the waves," or Dionysus' statement that he came to Hades "in order
that the city might be saved and present her choruses" (704; 1419).
Moreover, as said earlier the shape of the plot follows a tragic rather
than a comic scheme, in that Dionysus does not seek to identify himself with the boundless, but to extract the truth from it, while the
prime comic vehicle, speech, is clearly rejected in the person of Euripides. These facts, together with the air of gravity imposed by the
ever present Eleusinian theme and a chorus of not very comic Mystae,
prompt the suspicion that the choice of Aeschylus and his return to life
are not so brightly cheerful as they might seem.

Dionysus puts the problem clearly in the line just quoted; he then
asks two questions, one very specific, the second general. A degree of
ambiguity hovers over the answers of the two poets, and one could
make the case that from the practical point of view Euripides' replies
are at least as helpful as those of Aeschylus. Asked for his opinion of
Alcibiades, Euripides states in three crisp, epigrammatic lines the perfectly clear opinion that Alcibiades is a self-interested traitor. His
advice for the ultimate safety of the city comes clad in a heavy robe of

nonsense, but it could be interpreted as embracing a sane idea, indeed much the same idea as is suggested in the parabasis, that salvation lies in placing the city in the hands of the better citizens. At least this is what he says when, at Dionysus' request, he stops talking about "winging Cleocritus with Cinesias," and devising sharp sophistic figures of speech, and states clearly (1446f.):

> If we distrust the citizens whom now
> We trust, and those whom we do not employ
> Employ again, perhaps we might be saved.
> For if in our present ways we fare ill, why
> Might not salvation lie in the reverse?

In summary, then, Euripides recommends expelling Alcibiades (which had already been done), and turning the government over to the better citizens, whoever they may have been (which the chorus also recommends); he seems to be quite on the side of the angels. One might well expect him to win on these grounds. Instead, partly perhaps just because he has answered in apparently practical terms, and therefore has answered for the world of the present, Dionysus hails him as Palamedes, the type of clever speaker, and turns to Aeschylus.

The answers of Aeschylus are very different. Whether or not Euripides' counsels may be considered feasible, his rival's seem at a considerable remove from practicality. About Alcibiades he says (1431f.):

> Best if the city rear no lion's whelp,
> But if it rear one, it must serve his ways.

Are we to conclude that Aeschylus favored the recall of Alcibiades? Since the real Aeschylus could never have had any thoughts at all about Alcibiades, Aristophanes is quite free to make his character say what he pleases. Yet it is unlikely that he would put into the mouth of the archpoet of Athenian democracy a statement in favor of "serving the ways" of this flagrant would-be tyrant, while attributing the opposite view to the somewhat antidemocratic Euripides. Aristophanes has something else in mind, something which could hardly be stated outright. There can be little doubt that the image of the lion's whelp, as some have observed, comes from the famous chorus of the *Agamemnon* (717f.; 727f.):

> Once in his home a man raised up
> A lion's whelp, at life's beginning
> Udderless nurseling, gentle and mild
> To the children, a sport for elders . . .

In time he showed his nature, sprung
From his forebears; paying his fosterers thanks,
Unbidden he makes his feast
In reckless sheep slaughter.

This lion cub is usually taken to stand for Helen, who came at first as a delight to the Trojans, and then caused their destruction; more likely it is Paris, whom the oracle bade Hecuba not to rear when he was born. In either case, however, the meaning is the same: destruction wrought from within. The Trojans "served the ways" of the lion cub with well-known results, and Aeschylus is darkly indicating that the city has nursed its own doom. Whether Aristophanes actually thought Alcibiades responsible is immaterial; the analogy between him and Paris provided a way to put this indirect prophecy into the mouth of Aeschylus.

In response to the question of how to secure the city's safety, Aeschylus is at first unwilling to say anything until he gets back to earth. Dionysus, however, presses him, using a formula of prayer to the dead, and is answered with these words (1463f.):

When they shall think the enemy's land their own,
And their own land the enemy's, ships their resource,
And their resources mere resourcelessness.

To complete the sentence, we must understand that the Athenians will be saved only when they do these things; but what is Aeschylus saying? His first stipulation is nothing more than a restatement of the policy of Pericles, now dead for twenty-five years, that the Athenians should allow the enemy their will of Attica, while they themselves harry the Peloponnesian coasts. Whatever the merits of this policy in 431, in 405 it was somewhat outmoded, to say the least. The sole surviving fleet could not be spared to harry the Peloponnesus, since it was needed to keep the Pontic grain route open against the Spartan-Persian coalition; as for letting the Spartans have their will of Attica, they had had it with little or no question since the fortification of Decelea in 413. If Aeschylus is proposing to resurrect Periclean policy, he must first resurrect Periclean Athens. As for the statement about the ships as resource, it is a clear reference to the Battle of Salamis, when the Athenians, led by Themistocles, literally abandoned all their resources except their ships. Once more, this policy, so salutary in 480, could not strike anyone as very practical in 405; from the literal point of view, Euripides' advice is much better.

But Aristophanes is not dealing with literal facts and policies, for all the apparent immediate concern with politics in this play. The quest was for the truth about Athens, her culture and her corporate selfhood, and it is perhaps no wonder that Aeschylus hesitates to speak. When he invokes the two great leaders of the imperial democracy, both long since in their graves, and says that only by their counsels will Athens be saved, he has told the truth, and a very sad truth. The great days are over; the city will not be saved; it must serve the ways of the lion's whelp. Dionysus has come for the truth, and now he has it. His reply is a problem: "Yes," he says, "but only the judge will swallow that." It is impossible to take this line, as is usually done, as a reference to the embezzlement of public revenue by the judiciary (1466); by the judge he must mean himself, and by "swallow" he must mean "believe." Aeschylus has spoken the truth, but no one will believe it except Dionysus, the god who has taken upon himself the responsible journey into Hades; for truth is known only when it is experienced.

So the resurrection of Aeschylus is really a paradox. Like the *Frogs* as a whole, it is far less cheerful than it seems. Though it follows externally the comic design in achieving the impossible, the lack of revelry, the gravity of the issue, and the sorrowful tone betray the underlying lament. Aeschylus departs for the upper world to the solemn roll of dactylic hexameters, the rhythm of heroic and oracular poetry; the effect is funereal. The familiar comic theme of rejuvenation, though not totally absent, has been supplanted for the most part by the theme of resurrection; but the indispensable condition for resurrection is death. Whatever the Mysteries promised by way of immortality, it does not seem that they envisioned so simple a return from the grave as this of Aeschylus. To resurrect the poet in this sense, and in the terms used, comes close to confessing that he is gone forever.

And yet, though that threnodic tone is distinctly audible, it is not the whole truth, for the paradox goes further. What seems to be a settled dialectic of true and false, steadfast and variable, "generative" and sterile, is all seen through the veil of an inclusive ambiguity, created by a number of passages which invert, or even break down, the distinction between life and death. The third equivocation which Dionysus turns back upon its author at the end is the line: "Who knows if life be death or death be life?" (1477). Earlier in the play Aeschylus had included this famous remark in the list of Euripides' sins, presumably as a piece of philosophic twaddle; but it nonetheless summarizes one of the most poignant motifs of the play. The whole quest is paradoxical—to journey into death to find a life-giving poet, and to find the vivifying cultural principle in a voice which had been silent for fifty years. The scene with the corpse at the beginning sets the tone. He wants two drachmas to carry the luggage to Hades. Dionysus offers nine obols, and the corpse replies: "I'll get out of my grave first" (176f.). This scene might pass for a bit of macabre but merry nonsense, save that it agrees with so much else. The lower world and the upper, specifically Athens, are deliberately confused: the light that shines on the Mystae is like the light that shines in the upper world; Theseus is responsible for the two-obol payment in Hell; the better element in the infernal population is as scarce as it is in Athens; most pointedly, the chorus refers to the living as "the upper dead" (424). Here as elsewhere, Aristophanes seems to feel and exploit the force of the corrosive and paradoxical questioning that characterized the new intellectualism; distinctions once clear are no longer clear, and reality totters. When Dionysus quotes Euripides' line, he adds another, of almost nihilistic mockery, which seems to imply, "Who knows if anything be anything?" He might be just making fun of Euripides, but in fact, how does one know? The age of philosophy had arrived.

> For we alone possess the sun
> And joyous light,

sing the Mystae (455f.). Amid all the shifting sands, a rallying point is perhaps to be found in the Eleusinian theme. The Mysteries seem to bridge the gap between the two worlds, so that the distinction, if there is any, no longer matters. But within the play, the Eleusinian theme has gained, as we have seen, the added significance of public and cultural, as well as personal, redemption. In this respect, the Mysteries connect with the view of tragedy (and comedy) characteristic of the play: the city must be safe *and stage choruses.* Poetry, too, has her mysteries, and the *orgia* of the Muses, the Bacchic rites of "bull-eating Cratinus," and the *teletai* of Dionysus are all celebrated by the chorus as holy rituals, somehow analogous to the Mysteries of Demeter herself. Perhaps it is simply that poetry, in particular the dramatic poetry of Athens, is the public symptom of what the Mysteries revealed in secret, the inviolable life of the spirit. In any case, on true poetry the sun does not cease to shine, as Aeschylus said (866f.):

> *Aesch.:* I didn't want to stage a contest here.
> The fight between us isn't fair.
> *Dion.:*   Why not?
> *Aesch.:* Because my poetry did not die with me,
> His did; he has it handy to declaim.

With nineteen plays extant against Aeschylus' seven, the ghost of
Euripides may now console himself a little for this unkind cut; but in
405 he had to play the role assigned him. In Aeschylus Aristophanes
found a figure through whom he could say, "Athens is falling; her
meaning is immortal."

The Death of Tragedy

by Bruno Snell

In the year 406 B.C., immediately after the death of Sophocles and Euripides, Aristophanes in one of his most impressive comedies made the astonishingly correct prediction that tragedy had died with them. And indeed tragedy lay dead for about two thousand years. In his play, the *Frogs*, Aristophanes also tells us what, in his opinion, caused tragedy to expire. At the end of the comedy, the chorus sings:

> Right it is and befitting
> Not, by Socrates sitting,
> Idle talk to pursue,
> Stripping tragedy-art of
> All things noble and true.[1]

The art had in fact been stripped of its very existence, and it cannot be denied that philosophy was responsible for its destruction. Of this Aristophanes, with his extraordinary insight, was fully aware. Socrates whose name he mentions in this connection was the most prosaic of all Greeks. Only as a very old man, when shortly before his death he made a last conscientious appraisal of his life, he tried his hand at the writing of verse, much as if he wished to fill a gap in the sum total of his experience before the end overtook him. Socrates managed to side-track the young Plato from the composing of tragedies, and to make him into a philosopher and a writer of prose. But the poet whom Aristophanes has in mind when he describes him as sitting by Socrates and spelling the ruin of tragedy is Euripides. The plot of the *Frogs* leads us into the underworld, where we come upon Euripides engaging in a mighty contest against Aeschylus for the place of honor among poets.

"The Death of Tragedy," by Bruno Snell. Excerpted from the chapter "Aristophanes and Aesthetic Criticism" in The Discovery of the Mind *(Cambridge: Harvard University Press, 1953; Oxford: Basil Blackwell & Mott, Ltd., 1953), by Bruno Snell, translated by T. G. Rosenmeyer. Copyright © 1953 by the President and Fellows of Harvard College. Reprinted, without scholarly notes, by permission of Harvard University Press and Basil Blackwell, Oxford.*

[1] Lines 1491-95, tr. B. B. Rogers, as will be the following quotations from the *Frogs*.

In a mixture of burlesque and grandiose exaggeration Aeschylus appears as a crude unsophisticated bard, heroic and belligerent, of whom it is said (822ff.):

> There will his shaggy-born crest upbristle for anger and woe,
> Horribly frowning and growling, his fury will launch at the foe
> Huge-clamped masses of words, with exertion Titanic uptearing
> Great ship-timber planks for the fray.

But Euripides who peopled his stage with beggars and strumpets knows how to defend himself (826ff.):

> But here will the tongue be at work, uncoiling, word-testing, refining,
> Sophist-creator of phrases, dissecting, detracting, maligning,
> Shaking the envious bits, and with subtle analysis paring
> The lung's large labor away.

The criticism which Aristophanes levels against Euripides is for the most part rather superficial; in no other fashion could his comedies have managed to reach the Attic theatre-goer and shake him out of his inertia. He does not flinch from inventing the most infamous allegations, and summarily condemns everything *modern*. Innovators and reformers of diverse loyalties are shown in his plays as a promiscuous band of gossips, knaves, and corrupters of young men. Whatever the differences between Euripides, Socrates, and the Sophists, in Aristophanes they are indistinguishable; their only activity consists in cleverly lining their pockets through the teaching of various tricks which are destined to wreck the healthy morality of the solid Athenian citizen, and to subvert the traditional structure of the State.

Aristophanes was unable to save the young generation. The best of them sat with Socrates, and while he was, in the eleventh hour, sensible of a void in his life, they were no longer troubled by such thoughts. Disregarding a handful of well-meaning dilettanti and a few vain virtuosos, the year in which the *Frogs* had its premiere became the turning-point after which the Greeks ceased to write stately verse. For one whole century prose reigned supreme. Plato, Aristotle, Theophrastus, Epicurus write their philosophical works, and Isocrates and Demosthenes lead oratory to its glorious heights. The only poetry of the fourth century which exerted an influence upon subsequent generations was the New Comedy, the bourgeois comedy of manners which Menander and his associates put on the stage, and which was far removed from that sublime poetic ideal for whose return Aristophanes clamored.

And yet, though the further development of poetry ran counter to the wishes and inclinations of Aristophanes, the ideas which he offered in the *Frogs* did not fall on sterile ground. They continued to live, albeit in a sense which Aristophanes did not desire, or even deem possible. Not poetry itself, but the judging of poetry, and aesthetic discussion, were affected by his pronouncements; even today's literary criticism is indebted to his influence. Some time passed, however, before the fundamental significance of his remarks was appreciated, and it was not until very much later that his peculiar orientation met with its share of approval.

There is some doubt how many of the ideas which are of interest to us here were formulated by Aristophanes himself, and which are the views of his contemporaries, or perhaps even the common heritage of his age. For myself I am inclined to believe that the personal contribution of Aristophanes in these matters was very substantial.

In his earliest dialogues Plato uses certain phrases which remind us of the *Frogs*. In the *Gorgias*, for instance (501ff.), it is taken for granted that tragedy aims only at the gratification of pleasure (*hedone*), and it is therefore characterized as an adulatory art (*kolakeia*) whose objective cannot be genuine virtue (*arete*). Here Plato echoes Aristophanes, though naturally he modifies his thought. Both of them measure tragedy by the standard of morality. This moralization of poetry we owe to Aristophanes; its first exposition as a doctrine, as a deliberate program, occurs in the *Frogs*. Even in his earlier plays he holds Euripides up to ridicule, but it is in his *Frogs* that his criticism becomes a matter of principle. He accuses him of corrupting the Athenians, poisoning the patriotic spirit of the citizenry, and advancing the cause of immorality. The long dead Aeschylus, solemn and respected, is introduced for the sake of contrast. He had answered to a moral demand: that genuine poetry make better men of us (1008ff.). The Sophists also claimed to be able to make men better, but according to the view of Aristophanes they merely corrupted the youth. This judgment he transfers to Euripides; as he expresses it in the *Frogs,* it is the task of poetry to make men into valiant and useful citizens, but Euripides served to dissipate and destroy them. Aristophanes found it easy to equate the poets and the Sophists for the reason that the latter themselves, forced to canvass the public under a cloak of moderation and respectability, sought to connect their program of adult education with the training given to the young. The children were taught from the writings of Homer, Hesiod, Orpheus, and Musaeus; these were the writers, Hippias says in the introduction to one of his treatises (fr. 6), whose teachings it was necessary to summarize, to deepen, and to expand. We may assume, of course, that elsewhere he mentioned other writers in addition to the four.

Hippias, to be sure, does not yet regard it as the fundamental purpose or the chief function of the poets that they make men better. This version of the idea is coined by Aristophanes: the poets were teachers —Orpheus of the mysteries and rites, Musaeus of medicine and oracles, Hesiod of agriculture, the divine Homer of honor and glory (1032ff.)— and for adults they still play the same role as the school-master does for the children (1055). Even today Aristophanes is the key witness of those who hold that education is the basic concern of the arts, and of all culture in general. Plato makes this moral precept his own; his appointment of Socrates to be the judge of what is good would no doubt have startled Aristophanes. Against this philosophical axiom Plato, in the *Gorgias,* sets the empirical finding that tragedy merely appeals to the pleasure of the senses (*hedone*); with that he opens the door to endless discussions which via Horace continue well into the eighteenth century: the debate whether the proper task of poetry is *prodesse* or *delectare,* to profit or to please.

When Plato, with the moralization of poetry as his point of departure, eventually bans all poetic art from his State, he simply accepts the consequences of those ideas which first emerge in the *Gorgias.* Obviously Aristophanes is under no such constraint; he has no desire to preach a gospel of aesthetics, but merely to set off against a superior foil the poetry which he has come to hate. He chooses the charge of immorality because it is ruder and more effective than most others. It is evident, therefore, that Plato could not abstract a true theory of art from the *Frogs.* All he could get from it were certain hints and suggestions. Nor does Aristotle, in his *Poetics,* pay specific attention to the play. Years passed before the theorists began to take note of a distinction which Aristophanes had made to bring into sharp focus the contrast between Aeschylus and Euripides.

*   *   *

It is, of course, difficult to see how this theoretical interest in the good could have sustained the creation of tragedies or any other poetry. Attic tragedy breathed its last with Euripides, and Socrates bears the blame for its death. But at the same time he brought about the birth of something new: Attic philosophy. The judgment of Aristophanes is correct, but let us not be mistaken about him. He is a romantic reactionary who refuses to give up what is already lost, and, instead of welcoming the new, mourns the passing of the old.

His moral objections, however, are entirely unjustifiable. It will not do to accept a traditional code as the only possible morality, and to take it for granted that a decent citizen may do nothing except what is sanctioned by the established rules of religion, State, and family. Aristophanes fails to understand that a man's opposition to the traditions, and his appeal to another authority—be it reason or the voice of conscience—are fully as moral as obedience to custom; some have since considered it an even higher type of morality. As long as this new notion of justice is a matter of genuine conviction it will manifest itself not merely as an isolated sentiment, but as a persuasion common to many.

PART TWO

View Points

Margarete Bieber: A Portrait of Aristophanes

Aristophanes amused his public, but not the leading and influential persons, whom he lampooned. His type of comedy was early supplanted by new forms or even by the return to more primitive forms, from which he had evolved his masterpieces. The poet, therefore, never received an honorary statue, as did the tragic poets and the poets of New Comedy. We possess no contemporary portrait of Aristophanes. Many scholars including myself believe, however, that we have an excellent imaginary portrait of the poet. It was created in the Hellenistic period, probably as a companion piece to the portrait of Menander, with whom some Roman double herms couple him. Aristophanes is depicted as an older man, whose beginning baldness is hidden by some strands of hair falling irregularly onto his forehead. He looks coarse and unkempt. The beard has only irregular tufts, brow and cheeks are furrowed, the skin of the neck is crumpled and sacks of flesh hang below the deeply sunk eyes. The Hellenistic inventor of this portrait knew, however, how to express in these masterly rendered outer forms the intelligence and fiery expression, indicating the sincere striving of Aristophanes for high social and political ideals, and the disappointment in his failure to accomplish his goals.

"A Portrait of Aristophanes." From The History of the Greek and Roman Theater, *second edition (Princeton: Princeton University Press, 1961), by Margarete Bieber. Copyright © 1939, 1961 by Princeton University Press. Reprinted by permission of the publisher.*

Benjamin Bickley Rogers: Victory at Arginusae

The victory of Arginusae was the result of an almost unexampled effort on the part of the Athenian people. Conon, their most brilliant officer, had been defeated at Mitylene, and was closely blockaded there.

"Victory at Arginusae." From the introduction to The Frogs of Aristophanes *(London: G. Bell & Sons, Ltd., 1919), the Greek text revised, second edition, with a translation into corresponding meters, introduction, and commentary by Benjamin Bickley Rogers. Reprinted, without notes, by permission of G. Bell & Sons, Ltd.*

One trireme managed to run the blockade, and bring news of his peril to Athens. The Athenians received the intelligence in a spirit worthy of their best traditions. All classes at once responded to the call with hearty and contagious enthusiasm. In thirty days a fleet of 110 triremes, fully equipped and manned, was able to put to sea. The knights had emulated the devotion of their forefathers (as recorded in the parabasis of the comedy which bears their name), and volunteered for service on the unaccustomed element. The very slaves had been induced to join by the promise of freedom and, what was even more than freedom, the privileges of Athenian citizenship. Further triremes, as the fleet went on, were obtained from the islands, till it finally reached a total of more than 150 vessels. These exertions were rewarded by a victory which if it was the last, was also the most considerable of all that were gained by the Athenians during the Peloponnesian War. And the slaves who fought in the great battle were admitted to be free Athenian citizens on the same liberal terms as had been granted to the Plataeans who had escaped from their beleaguered city some one and twenty years before. They were enrolled in Athenian tribes and demes and enjoyed all the privileges of Athenian citizens, they and their sons after them for ever; save only that the individuals first enfranchised were not eligible for certain hereditary priesthoods (such as those of the Eumolpidae, the Eteobutadae, and the Ceryces), nor yet for the office of Archon. This exception was right and proper. It would have been very unpalatable for an Athenian to see a man who had been brought up altogether outside the Athenian traditions, and still more so for a master to see his former slave, occupying the supreme position of Archon. Yet even these excepted offices were not withheld from the children of the Plataean, or of the slave, even though they were born before their father acquired the Athenian citizenship.

The wholesale conversion of loyal slaves into free Athenian citizens, which met with the warmest approval of Aristophanes, readily lent itself to comic humor; and throughout the play, whenever he alludes to the battle of Arginusae, this incident is sure to crop up. In the *epirrhema*, which we have already discussed, *"Shall we give the franchise,"* ask the Chorus, *"to slaves who have fought but one battle, and yet withhold it from freeborn Athenians, who, and whose fathers before them, have fought so many battles for Athens?"* *"O why was I not at the sea-fight?"* cries Xanthias to his master (33-34), *"I would have bidden you go and be hanged; I would have snapped my fingers at your commands."* *"I take no slave on my ferry,"* says Charon (190-91), *"unless he fought in the sea-fight,"* in which case, be it observed, he would not be a slave at all.

W. B. *Stanford:* The Lenaean Festival—The Audience

The Lenaean Festival

Every wise community has cheerful winter festivals to brighten the gloom of the darker and colder days. The Athenians had three winter festivals of Dionysos (the god of wine, energy, and growth). These were the Rustic Dionysia in December, the Lenaea at the end of January or beginning of February, and the Anthesteria later in February.

During these festivals the Athenians were accustomed to leave their work and enjoy themselves under the relaxing influence of Dionysos and his wine. The Lenaean Festival included competitions for writers of comedy. Normally five comedies, but during the stringencies of the Peloponnesian War only three, were performed. All free-born Athenians (except, presumably, young children) attended the theater, primarily as a religious duty but also in pleasant expectation of free and easy fun. Public business was suspended in the parliament and law courts; prisoners were released from jail; trade and work were forbidden. All came in holiday mood, as to a carnival or fiesta in Latin countries today; and many were—to put it mildly—exhilarated by wine.

The performances began in the morning and took place in the open air—in contrast with our modern indoor evening performances. Fresh-minded and relaxed, the Athenians watched the comedies in a setting of superb natural beauty. From where they sat or stood on the steep southerly slope of the Acropolis they could look across the plain of Attica to the southernmost slopes of Hymettos and the Saronic Gulf. But beyond this, if the air was clear, they could also see the territory of their Peloponnesian enemies.

The Audience

What kind of people were those Athenians in the Theater of Dionysos? Let us, in imagination, look round the audience at the first

"The Lenaean Festival" and *"The Audience."* From the introduction to Aristophanes: The Frogs, *second edition (London: Macmillan & Co., Ltd., 1963), by W. B. Stanford. Copyright © 1958 by W. B. Stanford. Reprinted, without notes, by permission of the author, St. Martin's Press, Inc., The Macmillan Company of Canada, Ltd., and Macmillan & Co., Ltd.*

production of *Frogs*. There in the front row are the principal magis-
trates and priests of the city—the Priest of Dionysos in the seat of
honor. Near them, perhaps, are the party politicians—the demagogues
and their supporters. They may well be wondering which of them
Aristophanes will choose to mock in his new play. (In fact he does
mock Archedemos, Cleophon, Theramenes, and others.) Over there,
looking, perhaps, rather scornful and fastidious, sit the followers of the
Sophists. Aristophanes will not spare them either. Other intellectuals
are here, too: philosophers (Socrates and young Plato probably among
them), playwrights (but Sophocles and Euripides died last year), his-
torians, orators, poets, literary critics, and wits. The last two with
their 'sniffy nostrils' (893) will be hard to please. They will demand
subtlety, originality, and a polished style before they approve of any
play.

In contrast with these sophisticated cityfolk, those less self-assured
people further back, with badly cut clothes and awkward gestures, are
from the country parts of Attica. In normal times they would be easy
enough to amuse. But they have a special reason now for being glum.
The Peloponnesian invaders have occupied most of the Attic countryside since 413, and these countryfolk have been cooped up in the city
for several years. If Aristophanes wants to make them laugh, he will
have to crack plenty of broad, earthy jokes and bring in amiable references to their beloved countryside with a chorus of, say, country frogs
or birds or wasps to make them feel at home. They will like it, too, if
he makes fun of the city people—and so he does.

Other groups will expect notice and sympathy, too: the city workers
suffering from high wartime prices; traders anxious about shortages
of supplies; aristocrats deploring the loss of their ancestral privileges
and properties; out-of-office politicians eager for revolution and reform;
and—a pathetic group this—those citizens who have lost their political
rights as the result of recent plots and counter-plots.

These will all want to feel, as they watch the play, that they are 'in
the picture,' that the playwright is at least sometimes on *their* side, and
that he can laugh *with* them as well as *at* them. And, as will be seen
in *Frogs*, Aristophanes does in fact show great skill in catering for all
these multifarious interests among the audience. In contrast his two
rivals in the dramatic competition had appealed, if we may judge
from the titles of their plays, to special sections of the audience—
Phrynichus in *The Muses* to those interested in literature, Plato in
Cleophon to the political factions. But Aristophanes, universal in his
appeal then and now, had something for everyone, and won the first
prize.

K. J. *Dover:* Comedy and Society

Not all the humor of Comedy is verbal, and not all the verbal humor is readily appreciated without effort. The analysis of humor is never popular, thanks to the superstition that a joke explained is no joke. Fortunately useful classificatory work has been done on some obvious types of humor in Comedy, but there is much in the Greek sense of humor and sense of fantasy which is elusive. The enjoyment of tremendous indecency in close conjunction with refined literary criticism no longer presents a serious problem, for the unparalleled restraint imposed on the written word by the convention of the nineteenth century has died the death of all excesses; contemplation of the cold and arrogant savageries which our own world perpetrates makes us turn with something like relief to Aristophanic lechery. For the understanding of those aspects of Comedy which are really alien to our own culture we cannot do better than look to the modern Greeks. Anyone who has seen dancing in a Greek village will not discount the final clause in *Wasps* 1524-30:

τὸ Φρυνίχειον ἐκλακτισάτω τις ὅπως ἰδόντες ἄνω σκέλος ὤζωσιν οἱ θεαταί.
[kick out, till all admire,
The Phrynichean kick to the sky;
That the audience may applaud,
as they view your leg on high.—B. B. Rogers]

On a more sophisticated level, there is hardly an incident, hardly even a phrase, in Nikos Kazantsakis' novel *Zorba the Greek* which has not an alien ring to ears which know only English, but no one who has read Aristophanes will raise his eyebrows at a remark such as 'Many are the joys of this world—women, fruit, ideas,' which the *New Yorker* picked out for sarcastic comment.

Though the attention paid to the audience's sense of humor has been scanty, much has been paid to its intellectual attainments, and it is commonly represented as sceptical in religion and intimately conversant with great poetry. The case for its scepticism rests primarily on its tolerance of the discomfiture of Poseidon in *Birds* and the discreditable antics of Dionysus in *Frogs.* Yet the conclusion that Athenian society in

"Comedy and Society" by K. J. Dover. From "Greek Comedy" in Fifty Years of Classical Scholarship, *ed. Maurice Platnauer (Oxford: Basil Blackwell & Mott, Ltd., 1954). Copyright © 1954 by Basil Blackwell & Mott, Ltd. Reprinted, without notes, by permission of the publisher.*

the late fifth century was in general sceptical of traditional religion is not easily reconciled with the evidence from other sources, and rests on a failure of the imagination. To understand pre-Christian religious attitudes requires a great imaginative effort, and those who make it are commonly regarded as impostors by those who cannot. The intimate association of the gods with the fabric of ordinary Greek life is something which might be better understood by a Papuan than by a bishop, and perhaps best of all by the medieval Christian, whose humor was full of casual blasphemy and prompt to interweave the comic and the tremendous. The fact is that the Greek gods had human pleasures and understood laughter; at the right time and place they could take a joke.

The case for the literary discrimination of the Athenian audience rests on the fondness of Comedy for literary topics and above all for parody. But it has been remarked that criticism of poetry in Comedy tended to be criticism of the poet's person (real or conventionalized) rather than of his art; and the humor of para-tragedy lies not in the choice of the particular tragic passage but in the use of tragic language as such in a comic context. The audience could detect that tragedy was being parodied without identifying lines from *Telephus* or *Medea*, and the stance and voice of the actor would show them that it was there to be detected. Even if they recognized the original and remembered its source, it may be that the majority of the allusions in Comedy are allusions to lines which the poet knew from experience were widely disseminated, and to remember ἡ γλῶσσ' ὀμώμοχ' ἡ δὲ φρὴν ἀνώμοτος (my tongue has sworn but my mind has not) is not the same thing as forming critical judgment on *Hippolytus*. Again, the poet may often have amused himself by recondite allusions which he did not expect his audience to appreciate; experience of the modern 'little' revue suggests that the uninformed majority will readily join in the laughter of the few and feel more flattered than insulted by an appeal to their discrimination.

Attempts to use Comedy as evidence for Athenian society and economy are valuable and productive, but the material needs very cautious handling. It is not only that the closest attention must be paid to the context, for that is a necessary principle of all interpretation. The sociologist using Comedy must deal with two special difficulties, the autonomous comic myth and the nature of comic statement. The fidelity of Comedy to ordinary life can be overrated; as well as the farmer of real life, there is the conventional farmer of Comedy, and the two may differ. Comic conventions tend to lag behind the times; in the comic papers of our own day sergeant-majors wear waxed moustaches, countrymen chew straws, and dons spend their whole adult life in serene senility. In comic statement there is no room for judicious accuracy; it must be forceful and slick and capture the audience's interest.

* * *

⌐The common view of Aristophanes as a preacher has to contend with the coincidence that to judge from the fragments the other poets of Old Comedy all belonged to the same crusted minority. Croiset attempted to meet this difficulty by suggesting that Comedy was traditionally the favored art-form of the conservative, suspicious Attic farmers, and that its character and development were determined by the sympathies of this appreciative audience.

But the presentation of Aristophanes, to say nothing of other poets, as spokesman or instrument of a party or class is easier to sustain on a first reading than on a second. Any consistent picture of his views which can be constructed from snippets of chorus or dialogue, chosen without regard for speaker or context, can be confronted by different pictures constructed on the same principle. Aristophanes was a dramatist of genius; he had a keen eye for the absurdities inherent in all conflicts of temperaments and ideas, and he was concerned, *qua* dramatist, to exploit them. Thus in *Clouds* his purpose was not to persuade his audiences of the immorality of Socrates but to bring together Strepsiades, Pheidippides and Socrates, each in his own way an ass, and work out, with dramatist's logic, what happens.

Moreover, Comedy by its very nature makes certain demands on its practitioners. In Aristophanes, as in popular comedy of all ages, people are presented as they appear to the Common Man, who is tough but comfort-loving, shrewd but uneducated, caustic but unpolished, irreverent and intolerant of the unfamiliar. With the Common Man as foil, 'Euripides' and 'Socrates' are composite characters exhibiting the features popularly attributed to the intellectual, and their individuality is to some extent suppressed in order to secure their conformity to accepted comic types.

It may also be true that the good comic writer is almost inevitably committed to rebellion—or reaction; it does not matter which we call it—against the established order and the fashions and movements of his day. The same facet of his mind that makes him fertile in comic invention makes him sceptical and independent. Wit and cant do not live comfortably together, and for all its fierce virtues Athenian public life was not lacking in cant. ⌐

Gilbert Norwood: Farce in the *Frogs*

⌐The farcical scenes are not merely among the best he ever wrote:
they remind us for once of both Shakespeare and Molière by their
combination of splendid gusto and consummate finish.⌐ That scene
where the two landladies assail their supposed defaulting customer
reads like the germ of the verbal affray between Falstaff and "Dame
Partlet the hen" (*Henry IV*, Pt. I, III, iii). Moreover, like Sir John,
Heracles knows intimately the lower social life and the topography of
the capital: for "Hell is a city much like London" as Shelley said; or,
as Aristophanes implies (vv. 108 sqq.), like Athens. Molière excels
perhaps all other dramatists in the deftness wherewith he distils not
only much fun from a situation but (if one may dogmatize on such a
theme) literally all the fun. In this play the Greek approaches the
Frenchman. Consider that scene where Xanthias, once more disguised
as Heracles, is invited by Persephone to a banquet. Most playwrights,
and Aristophanes himself at the *Acharnians* level, would have made
Xanthias gleefully enter the palace, leaving Dionysus to pine through
the keyhole. A vastly richer effect is gained by causing Xanthias, amid
the stupefaction of all who know Heracles, to reply: 'Many thanks,
but I must decline.' A similar touch appears in the brawl with the
hostesses: after devouring mountains of provender and avoiding the
bill by a pretence of homicidal madness that sent Dame Partlet and her
colleague fleeing upstairs, the hero decamped—with the door-mats
under his arm (v. 567). Other instances may easily be observed in the
trial by scourging.

"Farce in the Frogs.*" From* Greek Comedy *(London: Methuen & Co., Ltd., 1931),
by Gilbert Norwood. Copyright 1931 by Methuen & Co., Ltd. Reprinted by permission of Methuen & Co., Ltd. and Hill and Wang, Inc.*

Henry David Thoreau: Frogs at Walden

Late in the evening I heard the distant rumbling of wagons over
bridges,—a sound heard farther than almost any other at night,—the
baying of dogs, and sometimes again the lowing of some disconsolate
cow in a distant barn-yard. In the mean while all the shore rang with
the trump of bullfrogs, the sturdy spirits of ancient winebibbers and
wassailers, still unrepentant, trying to sing a catch in their Stygian

"Frogs at Walden." From "Sounds," Chapter 4 of Walden, *by Henry David
Thoreau.*

lake,—if the Walden nymphs will pardon the comparison, for though there are almost no weeds, there are frogs there,—who would fain keep up the hilarious rules of their old festal tables, though their voices have waxed hoarse and solemnly grave, mocking at mirth, and the wine has lost its flavor, and become only liquor to distend their paunches, and sweet intoxication never comes to drown the memory of the past, but mere saturation and waterloggedness and distention. The most aldermanic, with his chin upon a heart-leaf, which serves for a napkin to his drooling chaps, under this northern shore quaffs a deep draught of the once scorned water, and passes round the cup with the ejaculation *tr-r-r-oonk, tr-r-r-oonk, tr-r-r-oonk!* and straightway comes over the water from some distant cove the same password repeated, where the next in seniority and girth has gulped down to his mark; and when this observance has made the circuit of the shores, then ejaculates the master of ceremonies, with satisfaction, *tr-r-r-oonk!* and each in his turn repeats the same down to the least distended, leakiest, and flabbiest-paunched, that there be no mistake; and then the bowl goes round again and again, until the sun disperses the morning mist, and only the patriarch is not under the pond, but vainly bellowing *troonk* from time to time, and pausing for a reply.

The New York Times: *Frogs* Still in the Political Swim 2,371 Years After Aristophanes

ATHENS, July 24, [1966]—Aristophanes this week proved to be as politically up-to-date as he was in 405 B.C., when he first presented his comedy the *Frogs* here. The play kept 4,500 spectators in the 1,800-year-old theater of Herod Atticus here on their political toes for two and one-half hours. When it was over, they gave it a standing ovation.

The *Frogs* was staged as part of this year's Athens Festival by Karolos Koun's avant-garde Art Theater, which some years ago was ousted from the same stage for a too-liberal interpretation of Aristophanes' *Birds*. One reason for that Government ban was that Mr. Koun represented a priest of the fifth century B.C. in Christian Orthodox garb. The production, nonetheless, scored a success in London last year. There were as many amusing anachronisms in the *Frogs* this week, and the adaptation helped the spectators to transpose the remarks to Greek politics today.

In the play, Dionysus, the ancient god of wine and tragedy, travels to the underworld to bring a worthy poet back to Athens. There he sets up a contest between the dead playwrights Euripides and Aeschylus for the privilege of returning to life. Although Dionysus weighs the verse of the poets on huge scales, the contest is won by Aeschylus for his views on the Athenian politics of the time, when the controversy was over the return of Alcibiades from exile.

Like most theater audiences here, those at these three performances were largely liberal and left wing. When a guard of Plutus, god of the underworld, curses Dionysus, mistaking him for Hercules, with "you fat-headed idiot, crook, miasma," the audience burst into cheers. The word "miasma" was used six months ago by King Constantine in an attack on Communism, with wide reactions. Later, where Aristophanes used the chorus to voice his theories on politics, the leftists in the audience applauded such words as "amnesty" (a familiar Communist slogan here) or "democracy."

Where Aristophanes compared "the usurpers of power" to copper coins that have displaced coins of pure gold, the audience laughed, taking it as support for its view that the present government has displaced the legitimate center government ousted last summer.

During the altercations between the poets, the leftists seemed to side with Euripides rather than with Aeschylus, who expounds something like what they would label "monarchist-fascist" theories. Aeschylus, from time to time, yielded something to please the liberal audience, but they refrained from applause, apparently fearful that he would come up with some hateful remark.

The production also took anachronistic liberties, such as offering remarks about taxi drivers. And just before the contest, Euripides poured himself a stiff drink from a Thermos. The *Frogs* was a striking success, and, perhaps for the first time, an ancient Greek comedy attracted enough spectators to fill the theater at the foot of the Acropolis.

Chronology of Important Dates

455 B.C.	Death of Aeschylus; first performance of a play by Euripides.
c. 450	Aristophanes born, probably at Athens.
431	Outbreak of the Peloponnesian War between Athens and Sparta.
427	Aristophanes' first play performed, the *Banqueters*.
425-21	Aristophanes' plays, the *Acharnians, Knights, Clouds, Wasps,* and *Peace,* performed.
415-13	The outset, engagement, and annihilation of Athens' Sicilian expeditionary force; Aristophanes' *Birds* performed 414.
413	Sparta occupies Decelea, exercising military control over all of Attica except Athens and Piraeus.
411	Successful revolt of the Four Hundred who establish an oligarchy and after four months are overthrown; Aristophanes' *Lysistrata* and *Thesmophoriazusae* performed.
406	Athenian naval victory at Arginusae; deaths of Euripides and Sophocles.
405	The *Frogs* performed; Athenian naval defeat at Aegospotami.
404	Athens surrenders to Sparta, ending the Peloponnesian War.
392-88	Aristophanes' last plays, *Ecclesiazusae* and *Plutus,* performed.
c. 388	Death of Aristophanes.

Notes on the Editor and Contributors

DAVID J. LITTLEFIELD, the editor of this volume, teaches English and Classics at Middlebury College, where he is Chairman of the Division of Humanities. He has written on Aristophanes and Ovid and is preparing a critical study of the *Frogs*.

DAVID BARRETT of the Bodleian Library has translated into modern English the *Wasps, Thesmophoriazusae,* and the *Frogs* in the Penguin Classics Series for stage production.

MARGARETE BIEBER was Professor of Archaeology and Director of the Archaeological Institute at Giessen University before coming to America, where she was associated with Barnard College, Columbia, and Princeton Universities.

MAURICE CROISET was Professor of Greek Language and Literature at the Collège de France and from 1911 to 1929 its President. He wrote on Demosthenes, Homer, Aeschylus, Sophocles, and ancient culture, as well as on Aristophanes, and he translated Plato. President of L'Association Guillaume Budé and of the Franco-Hellenic League, he was a member of the Academy of Inscriptions and Belles-Lettres. He died in 1935.

K. J. DOVER, Fellow of the British Academy, is Professor of Greek at the University of St. Andrews. In 1960 he was Visiting Lecturer at Harvard University.

G. M. A. GRUBE, Professor of Classics at Trinity College of the University of Toronto, is the author of important studies of Plato and Euripides, and, most recently, of *The Greek and Roman Critics.*

ÉTIENNE LAPALUS has been a member of the French School at Athens and Professor of Greek Language and Literature and Dean of the Faculty at Dijon. He is now Rector of the University of Clermont-Ferrand.

GILBERT MURRAY, the late Regius Professor of Greek at Oxford University, was a noted translator of classical drama, a prolific and influential literary historian and critic, and a vigorous commentator on British politics.

GEORGE E. MYLONAS directed excavations at Eleusis and Mycenae and was decorated by King Paul of Greece for his archaeological discoveries. A member of the Permanent Council of the International Congress of Prehistoric and Proto-historic Sciences, he is presently Professor of Art and Archaeology at Washington University in St. Louis.

GILBERT NORWOOD was Professor of Classics and Director of Classical Studies at University College, Toronto. Educated at Cambridge University, he was Sather Professor of Classical Literature at the University of California during 1943-44, and wrote widely on classical subjects. He died in 1954.

BENJAMIN BICKLEY ROGERS was a successful lawyer before deafness cut short a promising career in English politics and allowed him to return to classical studies. He devoted the last fifty years of a long life to his famous editions and translations of Aristophanes. He died in 1919.

CHARLES PAUL SEGAL has been a Fellow of the American Academy in Rome and at the Center of Hellenic Studies in Washington, D. C., and has taught at Harvard and the University of Pennsylvania. He has written on a variety of classical subjects, including Homer, Sophocles, and Pindar.

BRUNO SNELL, for thirty years Professor of Greek Language and Literature at the University of Hamburg, is the editor of Pindar and Bacchylides and author of studies on linguistics, Greek metrics, and *Poetry and Society*.

W. B. STANFORD, Fellow of Trinity College, Dublin, is Regius Professor of Greek in the University of Dublin. Editor of the works of Sophocles, Homer, and Aristophanes, he is widely known for his book, *The Ulysses Theme: A Study in the Adaptability of a Traditional Hero.*

LEO STRAUSS is Robert Maynard Hutchins Distinguished Service Professor of Political Science at the University of Chicago. His books range in subject matter from *Thoughts on Machiavelli* through *Persecution and the Art of Writing* to *Natural Right and History*. His most recent work is *Socrates and Aristophanes.*

HENRY DAVID THOREAU, the famous American essayist, poet, naturalist, and transcendentalist, was born in 1817 and died in 1862.

MATTHEW TIERNEY was for more than twenty years Professor of Greek at University College, Dublin, before becoming its President in 1947. He served as a Member of the Irish Parliament (*Dáil Éireann*) from 1925 to 1932 and as Vice-Chairman of the Irish Senate (*Seanad Éireann*) from 1938 to 1944.

CEDRIC H. WHITMAN is Professor of Greek Literature at Harvard University. His recent studies of tragic heroism in Sophocles, epic heroism in Homer, and comic heroism in Aristophanes have been major contributions to the critical study of classic Greek literature.

Selected Bibliography

Texts and Translations

Fitts, Dudley. *Aristophanes: Four Comedies*. New English versions of *Lysistrata, the Frogs, the Birds,* and *Ladies' Day (Thesmophoriazusae)*. New York: Harcourt, Brace, & World, Inc., 1962. A Harvest paperback. An excellent translation in modern American idiom.

Lattimore, Richmond. *Aristophanes: The Frogs*. In *The Complete Greek Comedy,* edited by William Arrowsmith. Ann Arbor: The University of Michigan Press, 1962. An excellent translation in modern American idiom.

Rogers, Benjamin Bickley. *The Frogs of Aristophanes*. The Greek text edited and revised, with introduction, commentary, and translation into corresponding meters; second edition. London: G. Bell & Sons, Ltd., 1919. Rogers' Greek text and translation appear—with very limited apparatus—in the Loeb Classical Library, *Aristophanes,* II; his translation is also available in *Five Comedies of Aristophanes,* an Anchor paperback.

Stanford, W. B. *Aristophanes: The Frogs*. The Greek text edited and revised, with introduction, commentary, index, and bibliography; second edition. London: Macmillan & Co., Ltd., 1963. An excellent modern 'school' edition.

Further Reading

Cook, Albert. *The Dark Voyage and the Golden Mean*. New York: W. W. Norton & Company, Inc., 1966. First published in 1949. Cook presents a novel theory of comedy in chapters 1 and 2 and in chapter 3 interprets Aristophanes within its perspective.

Cornford, Francis Macdonald. *The Origin of Attic Comedy*. Edited with foreword and additional notes by Theodore H. Gaster. Garden City, New York: Doubleday-Anchor Books, 1961. First published in 1914, Cornford's theory is no longer widely held, but his lively intelligence is still vital.

Ehrenberg, Victor. *The People of Aristophanes: A Sociology of Old Attic Comedy*. Second edition, corrected for paperback publication. New York:

Schocken Books, 1962. Much valuable information on the Athenian world of Aristophanes.

Gomme, A. W. "Aristophanes and Politics," *More Essays in Greek History and Literature*. Oxford: Basil Blackwell & Mott, Ltd., 1962. Reprint of a 1938 essay which insists on the primacy of Aristophanes' art.

Guthrie, W. K. C. *The Greeks and Their Gods*. Boston: Beacon Press, Inc., 1955. Chapter 6, "Dionysus," is an excellent overview of the nature and roles of this enigmatic god.

Jaeger, Werner. "The Comic Poetry of Aristophanes," Book II, Volume I, of *Paideia: The Ideals of Greek Culture*. Translated by Gilbert Highet; second edition. New York: Oxford University Press, Inc., 1945. A great scholar-critic's view of Aristophanes as a teacher.

Lever, Katherine. *The Art of Greek Comedy*. London: Methuen & Co., Ltd., 1956. Chapters 3, 4, and 5 examine Aristophanes as a servant of Dionysus, a comic dramatist, and a comic poet.

Pickard-Cambridge, Sir Arthur W. *Dithyramb, Tragedy, and Comedy*. Second edition; revised by T. B. L. Webster. Oxford: The Clarendon Press, 1962. Chapter 3, "The Beginnings of Greek Comedy," has a useful "Excursus: On the Form of the Old Comedy."

Webster, T. B. L. *Greek Theatre Production*. London: Methuen & Co., Ltd., 1956. A scholarly examination of all manner of evidence which bears upon the subject.